Redefining American Identity

Redefining American Identity

From Cabeza de Vaca to Barack Obama

Ben Railton

palgrave
macmillan

First published in 2011 by PALGRAVE MACMILLAN® in the United States—a division of St. Martin's Press LLC, 175 Fifth Avenue, New York, NY 10010.

Where this book is distributed in the UK, Europe and the rest of the world, this is by Palgrave Macmillan, a division of Macmillan Publishers Limited, registered in England, company number 785998, of Houndmills, Basingstoke, Hampshire RG21 6XS.

Palgrave Macmillan is the global academic imprint of the above companies and has companies and representatives throughout the world.

Palgrave® and Macmillan® are registered trademarks in the United States, the United Kingdom, Europe and other countries.

ISBN: 978-0-230-11206-3

Library of Congress Cataloging-in-Publication Data

Railton, Ben, 1977-
   Redefining American identity : from Cabeza de Vaca to Barack Obama / by Ben Railton.
      p. cm.
   Includes bibliographical references.
   ISBN 978-0-230-11206-3 (alk. paper)
      1. Cultural fusion—United States. 2. Cultural pluralism—United States. 3. Multiculturalism—United States. 4. National characteristics, American. 5. United States—Race relations. I. Title.

E184.A1R335 2010
305.800973—dc22   2010039063

A catalogue record of the book is available from the British Library.

Design by Scribe Inc.

First edition: April 2011

10 9 8 7 6 5 4 3 2 1

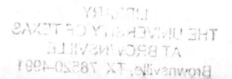

Contents

Preface

Transforming Our American Skin

The 1999 shooting of Amadou Diallo by four plainclothes New York City police officers, and even more significantly the responses to that tragedy across the political and cultural spectrum, seem to reveal, among many other tensions and divisions, the two fundamentally distinct and often opposed historical narratives at the center of the culture wars. Diallo was a 22-year-old Manhattan street peddler who had immigrated from the West African nation of Guinea two years earlier and was returning to his Bronx apartment building on the night of February 5. The four officers erroneously identified Diallo as the principal suspect in a rape case and, when he reached for his wallet, they mistook it for a gun and fired 41 shots at him, hitting him 19 times and killing him. The officers were tried for second-degree murder and other charges (in a trial that was moved to Albany) but were found innocent of all charges, and were likewise cleared of all wrongdoing by an internal investigation.[1] To proponents of a multicultural perspective on American identity and history, the incident and its aftermath form one particularly striking but not at all unique chapter in the long and ongoing narrative of official racism and violence, a telling reminder that what Jonathan Wallace called "officially condoned racism" is as present in late twentieth-century America as it was in (to cite only a few examples) the wars against Native Americans, the passage of the Chinese Exclusion Act, and the Wilson administration's support of the Jim Crow South. To proponents of a traditional perspective, on the other hand, such arguments are themselves, like the incident, simply indicative of post-1960s rifts in the nation's once-unified identity and community, rifts exemplified and exacerbated by multiculturalism and its advocates; it was in this vein for example, that Pat Buchanan would later attribute Al Sharpton's "stirring up mob protests" after the officers' acquittal to his ongoing role as a "chief incendiary" and "demagogue" who "plays the race card [because he] has no other card to play."

As has far too often been the case in culture-war conflicts, few commentators on either side of this division seemed to recognize that the five key players in the shooting, despite their obvious differences in identity and power (among other factors), were almost certainly linked and motivated by a shared and significant human emotion: fear for their lives. It is in that vein that the first two verses and repeated chorus of the most famous (and controversial[2]) artistic response to the shooting, Bruce Springsteen's song "American Skin (41 Shots)" (2001), attempt both to represent with a great deal of sympathy and to find the common ground between the perspectives on either side of the incident. The first verse's second-person subject is a police officer who, having fired his share of the titular shots, finds himself "kneeling over [Diallo's] body in the vestibule / praying for his life"; the second verse's speaker is an African American mother who implores her young son to "understand the rules" of interacting with the police; and each addressee is thus explicitly implicated in and threatened by the chorus's repeated acknowledgment that "you can get killed just for living in / your American skin." The pronoun usage brings together these two very disparate individuals—a white New York police officer and a young African American schoolchild—and makes clear that for both of them, in another of the chorus's key phrases, these dark realities can seem very centrally to comprise "your life."

If the song's unifications of these seemingly opposed individuals and perspectives ended there, they would be meaningful but bleak, a rather pessimistic vision of a nation linked by shared dangers and fears. But the final verse builds on and amplifies these earlier images, in three significant ways. It begins with the same two lines as the opening verse: "41 shots and we'll take that ride / Across this bloody river and to the other side," and here, after the song's 14 prior second-person pronouns, the "we" feels especially meaningful, a return to (and subsequent extension of) a communal perspective and future. The next line, "41 shots, got my boots caked in this mud," makes clear that the song's speaker sees himself as very much a part of that community, not only through his attempts to speak for the policeman and the mother but also in his own identity and life. And then, in the song's most complex and beautiful lines, he expresses just how fully interconnected that community's identities are: "We're baptized in these waters / And in each other's blood." That final "blood" certainly recalls the bloody river that had flowed out of Diallo and could flow from any of the song's protagonists at any time, but I believe that these lines also transcend both such tragic violence and the justifiable but damaging fears that it can produce, arguing instead for a shared, communal American identity that is anything but skin-deep, one in which we are fundamentally linked—baptized, even defined—by interconnections at our very core. Significantly, these are the only two lines in the song's verses that are echoed by all the band's members, a formal choice that emphasizes both the lines themselves and their message of communal identity and interconnection.

At its heart, this book represents an extended argument for precisely such defining American interconnections. In it I attempt to redefine American identity, to emphasize, in contrast to both the traditional and multicultural narratives, a third possibility for what has been at the core of America since the first moments of contact: cross-cultural transformation. By that phrase, I mean the way in which individuals and groups begin with relatively fixed cultural identities but experience complex shifts and transformations, across or through or toward other identities and cultures. My introduction lays out that definition, and its relationship to ongoing narratives and conversations in and outside of academia, at length. The chapters examine personal narratives of five individuals who experienced such transformations, one from each century of postcontact America; this approach allows for both in-depth analysis of each text and broader connections to other contemporaneous figures and texts, and between these eras and fundamentally American lives. And I conclude by analyzing Barack Obama's narrative of both his parents' cross-cultural transformations and his own status as a descendent of this heritage, a status that I believe all twenty-first-century

Americans share. As the responses to Obama's presidency, and especially the numerous and widespread attempts to define his identity as something distinctly outside of and even opposed to America have demonstrated, the project of recognizing and embracing our most complex and defining national identities—and thus transforming our American skin—has never been more necessary or relevant.

Acknowledgments

This book owes its existence to Fitchburg State University, in a wide variety of ways. I developed the germs of its ideas in conversation with students in American Literature I surveys in 2005, 2006, and 2007. I first articulated those ideas in a Graduate English Colloquium talk in the fall of 2007. They began to truly take shape when I was fortunate enough to deliver one of FSU's college-wide Harrod Lectures in the fall of 2008. And at every step of the way I have had the great fortune of sharing my thoughts and writing in progress with my colleagues, most especially those in the Faculty Reading Group; special thanks are due to Ian Williams, Aruna Krishnamurthy, and Michael Hoberman, but also and just as genuinely, thanks to Bornali Bhandari, Eric Budd, Chola Chisunka, Christine Dee, Sean Goodlett, Patrice Gray, Ben Lieberman, Frank Mabee, Carl Martin, and Joe Moser.

My circle of colleagues and conversation extends well beyond FSU, of course. For extended readings and responses, huge thanks to Carolyn Karcher, Miles Orvell, Steve Railton, and Larry Rosenwald. For crucial conversation, thanks as well to Heidi Kim, Steve Peterson, Ilene Railton, Jeff Renye, all my colleagues on the New England American Studies Association Council, and most especially Connie Tsao. For thorough support and consistent friendliness, thanks to Chris Chappell and Sarah Whalen at Palgrave and my copyeditor at Scribe. And for a very comfortable place to write, thanks to the staff of the Needham Public Library.

As I write in the conclusion, my multigenerational, cross-cultural family—both by birth and by marriage—is my constant source of inspiration, intellectually as in every other way. Most of all, this book is dedicated to the two best arguments I can possibly imagine for cross-cultural identities: Aidan and Kyle.

Introduction

Defining Transformations

James Davison Hunter opens his seminal *Culture Wars: The Struggle to Define America* (1991) with a series of interviews that he designates "Stories from the Front," and the first such voice is particularly telling. The interviewee, Chuck McIlhenny, is a Presbyterian pastor and conservative political activist in San Francisco, and the explicit occasion for his interview is a 1990 ballot initiative in that city that would allow unmarried couples (straight or gay) to register their relationship as a "domestic partnership." But as McIlhenny makes clear, his position on that particular issue is intimately connected to a broader perspective both on America's founding and historical identity and on the threats it faces in the late twentieth century. As Hunter paraphrases McIlhenny's "view of American history," "the Lord has blessed our nation over the centuries because our cultural heritage was Christian," but places like San Francisco are "rejecting that heritage," resulting in nothing less than a "fight between a biblical morality and the new morality" with the nation's soul and future at stake (7–8). McIlhenny does not spell out to Hunter exactly how he'd define the perspective of his opponents, those rejecting the Christian heritage in favor of the new morality; but many of the era's most vociferous and vocal advocates of that heritage were significantly more willing to provide such a definition. Exemplifying those advocates is cultural critic Alvin Schmidt, whose *The Menace of Multiculturalism: Trojan Horse in America* (1997) extends and amplifies McIlhenny's historical views. America "is a land whose people always believed they were 'one nation under God' and whose people said 'in God we trust,'" Schmidt argues, adding that "countless Americans believed that their nation was the 'Promised Land,' the land that God selected and preserved for them. Evidence for this belief is not lacking" (7). And as Schmidt's title highlights, he believes that the manifold forces and ideas that constitute the concept of multiculturalism have been at the forefront of the assault on that core, unifying historical identity: he surveys the contemporary landscape and notes that "many things in American culture—and some are already the result of multiculturalism's influence—are incompatible with the traditional Euro-American culture. It is the Euro-American culture that has made America great, and it is this culture that multiculturalism stands to destroy" (xiii).

Ronald Takaki opens his magisterial *A Different Mirror: A History of Multicultural America* (1993) by narrating a personal encounter with precisely that historical perspective. On his way to "a conference on multiculturalism," he is asked by a cab driver "how long [he has] been in this country"; Takaki recognizes that the cabbie has "a narrow but widely shared sense of the past—a history that has viewed American as European in ancestry," but notes in reply that his "family has been here, in America, for over a hundred years" (1). Moreover, he transitions directly from recounting that personal exchange and heritage into elucidating the historical perspective that provides his book's defining concept and purpose: his argument that "America has been racially diverse since our very beginning on the Virginia shore, and this reality is increasingly becoming visible and ubiquitous" (2–3); and his corresponding plan to "study the American past from a comparative perspective," in the hopes that "through their narratives about their lives and circumstances, the people of America's diverse groups [will be] able to see themselves and each other in our common past" (6–7, 16). His book demonstrates both the historical and cultural breadth of that comparative, multicultural project: Takaki begins with a section titled "Before Columbus" and closes with "Toward the Twenty-First Century," including in the course of that chronology multiple chapters focused on, among other cultures, Native Americans, African Americans, Irish Americans, Mexican Americans, Chinese Americans, and Eastern European/Jewish immigrants to the United States.

The culture wars that dominated much of America's public, political, and social discourse and life in the twentieth century's closing decades—and that certainly continue to play a central role into the early twenty-first century—often seem centered on a loose collection of distinct and generally very contemporary issues and controversies. Hunter identifies a selected but salient group of "such issues" on the first page of his preface: "abortion, gay rights, funding for the arts, women's rights, child-care policy, church and state litigation, multiculturalism, and court-packing" (xi). In that formulation, multiculturalism—and, implicitly, the belief in a Euro-American and Christian heritage that both Schmidt and Takaki identify as its alternative—is simply one of many such centers of debate. Yet I believe that those two historical perspectives, those opposing narratives of America's founding identity and history, are in fact at the heart of the divisions and debates that constitute the culture wars. For Hunter, the culture wars' fundamental divisions are "rooted in different systems of moral understanding," and in particular in two "polarizing impulses: the orthodox and the progressive" (42–43); his fellow cultural historian James Nolan similarly defines the debate as between "those who remain committed to an external, definable, and transcendent authority" and "those who are committed to a resymbolization of historic faiths according to the prevailing assumptions of contemporary life" (ix–x). Certainly many of the social movements that arose out of the 1960s (to cite one prominent example), and the subsequent changes in America that they helped produce, would seem directly linked to such differing impulses and beliefs; but it is difficult to argue that similar divisions and shifts have not occurred around the world over roughly the same period. It is thus particularly significant to identify the more specific, historical component to America's opposing perspectives: on the one hand, the Euro-American and Christian tradition, the narrative that seeks to define American history and identity as beginning, in every meaningful way, with the Puritan arrivals and culture; and on the other, the multicultural tradition, which takes a variety of forms (on which more below) but always foregrounds a narrative in which any national definition underscores all the groups and cultures that have been present and influential in America since the first moments of contact. Most of the culture wars' most heated recent controversies can be immediately and productively connected to those differing historical visions. For example, English should of course be the official national language if the Puritans comprise our founding culture, whereas the multiple languages spoken by Native Americans,

African slaves, and other European arrivals make us multilingual from the start, according to the multicultural view; the phrase "under God" should of course be included in the Pledge of Allegiance if our heritage is a Christian one, whereas a multicultural narrative would ask "Whose, and which, God? And what of Deists and atheists?" and so on.[1]

On both sides of this historical opposition there has been no shortage of scholars and commentators willing to delineate both their narrative's perspective and their sense of the alternative vision. Barbara Herrnstein Smith, defending multiculturalism in direct response to E. D. Hirsch's theory of a cultural literacy in which all American schoolchildren should be instructed, argues that "there is . . . no single, comprehensive macroculture in which all or even most of the citizens of this nation actually participate, no numerically preponderant majority culture in relation to which any or all of the others are 'minority' cultures, and no culture that, in Hirsch's terms, 'transcends' any or all other cultures" (71). African American scholars and writers Ishmael Reed and Amiri Baraka, in their respective contributions to the collection *Multi-America: Essays on Cultural Wars and Cultural Peace* (1997), edited by Reed, make even more explicit what constitutes that fictitious macroculture to which multiculturalism is opposed: Reed calls it a "WASP monoculturalism" (xvii); and Baraka's piece is titled "Multinational, Multicultural America versus White Supremacy" (391–94). Dean Harris introduces his edited collection, *Multiculturalism from the Margins: Non-Dominant Voices on Difference and Diversity* (1995), by arguing that opposition to the monocultural perspective stems from not only a recognition of multiple cultures but also a fundamental belief in the "liberating politics of difference" (xiii). And Kivisto and Rundblad, the editors of another collection, *Multiculturalism in the United States: Current Issues, Contemporary Voices* (2000), highlight both the movement's multiple focal points and its relationship to the Euro-American tradition in their introduction's section titles: European American Decline; African Americans; American Indians; Hispanic Americans; and Asian Americans.

Most of the prominent proponents of the traditional narrative have not been quite as willing as Schmidt to connect their historical emphasis explicitly to Euro-American and Christian cultures; but their varied frames and euphemisms line up closely with those cultures nonetheless. In Hirsch's *Cultural Literacy: What Every American Needs to Know* (1987) he identifies the education system's primary goal as "teaching children national mainstream culture" (24); his fellow educational commentator William Bennett, in his *To Reclaim a Legacy: A Report on the Humanities in Higher Education* (1984), had already laid out a bit more overtly what constituted that mainstream culture, arguing that "because our society is the product and we the inheritors of Western civilization, American students need an understanding of its origins and development, from its roots in antiquity to the present," and thus that "the core of the American college curriculum should be the civilization of the West" (9, 30). Dinesh D'Souza's *Illiberal Education: The Politics of Race and Sex on Campus* (1991) traces the rejection of that curricular mission, the ways in which "most American universities have diluted or displaced their 'core curriculum' in the great works of Western civilization to make room for new course requirements stressing non-Western cultures, Afro-American Studies, and Women's Studies" (5). Allan Bloom's *The Closing of the American Mind: How Higher Education Has Failed Democracy and Impoverished the Souls of Today's Students* (1987) initially argues that "the old view [of what it means to be an American] was that, by recognizing and accepting man's natural rights, men found a fundamental basis of unity and sameness" (27), but goes on to express the traditionalist and, at least implicitly, Eurocentric perspective that "the upshot of all this [multiculturalism] for the education of young Americans is that they know much less about American history and those who were held to be its heroes" (34). And Richard Bernstein's *Dictatorship of Virtue: Multiculturalism and the Battle for America's Future* (1994) makes plain the traditionalists' sense of the stakes in the abandonment of such educational priorities, arguing that "like it or not, there are certain cultural norms, certain things to know and do, a mastery of certain discourse, that is most likely to get people on the great engine of upward social mobility in the United States" (10).

My own position on the spectrum represented by these opposed historical narratives is a complex one: as a scholar and teacher who trained and works in the early twenty-first century, and as an Assistant Professor of Ethnic American Literature to boot, most of my intellectual and professional sympathies lie with multiculturalism; but my profound investment in the discipline of American Studies helps me to recognize both the ways in which each narrative captures certain aspects of America's history and identity (while eliding or minimizing others) and the significance of both narratives in American culture and thought for generations (if not centuries). Yet I also, and most importantly for this project, believe that an emphasis on the culture war divisions and clashes can obscure a subtle but ultimately fundamental similarity between the two historical narratives: the way in which they identify and focus on separate, distinct, clearly defined, and relatively static cultures. Viewed through that lens, the two narratives differ mostly in the number of focal points: one primary founding American culture in the traditional narrative; many coexisting founding cultures in the multicultural one. Because of that similarity, both narratives too often fail to do justice to the complexities and messiness and dynamic quality of the American past—and it is that dynamic quality in particular, which I connect to the concept of cross-cultural transformation and analyze throughout this book, that is truly at the core of America's complex and vibrant history and identity and culture, from the first century after contact to our twenty-first-century moment.

Scholars of the multicultural tradition might contend that my description of its historical narrative's focus on distinct and static cultures is accurate only regarding the movement's first iterations, and more exactly to the strand sometimes called *particularist multiculturalism*. That strand, which developed alongside the identity politics and ethnic studies departments of the 1970s and early 1980s, shared with those trends a separatist philosophy and purpose; Horace Kallen's essay "Democracy versus the Melting Pot: A Study of American Nationality" (1915) is often seen as an early model of this kind of multiculturalism, especially in Kallen's thorough critique of the melting pot ideal and his arguments for a cultural pluralism that depends precisely on "respect for ancestors [and] pride of race" in order to produce a nation that "realiz[es] the distinctive individuality of each *natio* that composes it." On the other hand, these dissenting scholars might point to what is sometimes called *cosmopolitan multiculturalism*, a later strand that includes its own version of the melting pot, an image of a unified national identity that is the composite yet more than just the sum of its many cultural parts. Randolph Bourne's essay "Trans-National America" (1916) is highlighted as an early model for this strand, particularly in Bourne's opposition to those who "insist that the alien shall be forcibly assimilated to that Anglo-Saxon tradition which they unquestionably label 'American'" and his depiction of a unified America that "is coming to be, not a nationality, but a transnationality, a weaving back and forth . . . of many threads of all sizes and colors" (86, 94). Yet both Kallen and Bourne were responding to a resurgent monocultural, Anglo-Saxon, Christian tradition (one that would result, for example, in the 1920s return of the Ku Klux Klan), and both opposed that narrative by highlighting the number of distinct threads out of which America is composed; if Kallen was most interested in the threads themselves, and Bourne in the pattern that they produce, that difference is to my mind one of emphasis rather than argument. Similarly, both the particularist and cosmopolitan multiculturalisms are centrally concerned with recognizing the multiplicity of founding American cultures; the cosmopolitan argues more explicitly for a unified national identity achieved through that multiplicity, while the particularist stresses the need for an understanding and celebration of the individual cultures, but that difference, while not insignificant, is one of purpose rather than of ideas or definitions.

It is precisely this central multicultural focus on the multiplicity of individual cultures that led three prominent American scholars in the early 1990s to critique multiculturalism; none of the three advocated for, and in fact all three critiqued, the traditional narrative, but nonetheless they shared a sense of the lack of national unity that multiculturalism might both portray and produce. Henry Louis Gates Jr. concludes the preface to *Loose Canons: Notes on the Culture Wars* (1992) by arguing that "today, the mindless celebration of difference for its own sake is no more tenable than the nostalgic return to some monochrome homogeneity" (xix); Arthur Schlesinger claims in *The Disuniting of America: Reflections on a Multicultural Society* (1992) that if "division into ethnic communities establishes the basic structure of American society and the basic meaning of American history," then "instead of a transformative nation with an identity all its own, America in this new light is seen as preservative of diverse alien identities" (16); and Robert Hughes notes in *Culture of Complaint: The Fraying of America* (1994) that "reading America is like scanning a mosaic. If you only look at the big picture, you do not see its parts—the distinct glass tiles, each a different color. If you concentrate only on the tiles, you cannot see the picture" (17). Each scholar shares a desire to find and articulate an alternative historical narrative, as expressed in Gates's hope that he has "contributed . . . to the search for a middle way" through which we can "collectively . . . forge a new, and vital, common American culture in the twenty-first century" (xvii, xix).

It is my contention, and this book's central argument, that such a vital and common American culture has been present throughout all the centuries of postcontact existence: a unifying national experience and identity that is neither composed of one macroculture nor divided into many individual cultures, but is instead explicitly defined by how all cultural identities and communities change in this dynamic and evolving new world. In this argument, what is truly at the core of America's identity and culture, from the exploration, settlement, and Revolutionary eras through the nineteenth and twentieth centuries and, ever more overtly and visibly (but not more fundamentally), into the twenty-first century, is the process I'm calling *cross-cultural transformation*, the way in which individuals and groups begin as part of fixed cultures but experience complex shifts and transformations, across or through or toward (but always in relationship to) other identities and cultures. In order to ground my conception and analysis of that process in specific experiences and identities, as well as in understanding of the choices made by individuals in portraying and reflecting on their experiences in written form, I develop in my main chapters extended readings of five American personal narratives. Each narrative highlights and represents an exemplary cross-cultural transformation from one of the centuries of American postcontact existence: Alvar Nuñez Cabeza de Vaca and sixteenth-century transformative explorations; Mary Rowlandson and seventeenth-century unsettling transformations; Olaudah Equiano and eighteenth-century revolutionary transformations; Sarah Winnemucca and nineteenth-century transformative expansions; Gloria Anzaldúa and twentieth-century transformative mixtures. In the conclusion I analyze Barack Obama's personal narrative of both his parents' cross-cultural transformations and his own evolving status and perspective as a hybrid descendent of that heritage, a status that makes Obama profoundly representative of twenty-first-century American identity and culture.

While those chapters and analyses flesh out my central concept and illustrate its variety of possible meanings and ramifications for American history, identity, and culture, a few additional words of clarification are no doubt in order at the outset. For one thing, I don't want to overstate the stability and unity of the individuals' cultural starting points, since all identities are of course composed of multiple elements and no ethnic or national community is perfectly (or even imperfectly) homogeneous. As David Goldstein notes in the introduction to a 2007 collection of essays on race, ethnicity, and hybridity in American literature, one of the most significant points that social scientists have established in their studies of racial identities and communities is that "diversity within categories far exceeds diversity between categories" (xvi); and certainly factors such as gender, age, class, profession, education, family background, religion, and sexuality (among others) influence each individual's relationship to his or her original culture. But I nevertheless do want to argue that those starting points are significantly more unified and static, and certainly more familiar and comfortable to the individuals, than either the transformative experiences or the hybrid American identities that they produce. Or at least that is how the individuals represent those starting points in their narratives—those representations could without question be oversimplified or mythologized or even falsified (as is potentially the case with Equiano's initial two chapters on his African homeland and experiences), but they are nonetheless how each author constructs his or her points of origin, and as such are profoundly telling about the partly imagined but highly influential communities in which the individuals are situated before their cross-cultural transformations.

Nor do I want to make it seem, in defining and framing this concept outside of my specific chapters and examples, as if cross-cultural transformation comprises a uniform set of experiences or meanings. Sometimes the transformations are transient, as with Rowlandson's return to her Puritan community and perspective at the end of her captivity or de Vaca's voyage back to Spain after his decade wandering in the New World; sometimes they're permanent, as with Equiano's thorough concluding embrace of a transatlantic and Christian identity. Sometimes they're painful or destructive, as evidenced by how much Winnemucca's mediating role as an interpreter distances her from her family and tribal connections and loved ones; sometimes they're uplifting and productive, as with Anzaldúa's ability to recognize and embrace all the components of her mestiza identity and future. Sometimes, perhaps most of the time in most Americans' lives, transformations go unremarked upon, happening so gradually or subtly as to seem inseparable from more familiar cultural identities or experiences. But sometimes they're noticed and captured in texts of all kinds; and the personal narrative, as I argue below, is a genre particularly well suited to capture the individual and communal complexities that constitute cross-cultural transformations. Precisely because of those complexities, an understanding of the specifics of the process is vital to developing a sense of what this cross-cultural identity represents and constitutes more broadly, both in each particular historical moment and in American history and culture more generally, and I try first and foremost to pay close, extended, analytical attention to those specifics and their textual representations throughout my chapters. But whatever the specifics, cross-cultural transformation is always dynamic, always renders untenable any fixed, absolute sense of America's culture or cultures as wholly distinct or static entities. If American identity is composed of—not just the product of (although that's what I'll argue about our twenty-first-century identity, as represented by Obama), but in fact centrally defined by—such transformations, then it is fundamentally both dynamic and hybrid, located in the movement across and space between cultures.

That definition of American identity locates my project in the midst of a number of parallel concepts from the last few decades. But before engaging with that ongoing scholarly conversation, I should acknowledge and respond briefly to three significant and understandable critiques that I can anticipate my argument receiving. Perhaps the most trenchant is that voiced by Christopher Newfield and Avery Gordon in the essay they contributed to their edited collection *Mapping Multiculturalism* (1996); they respond directly to scholars like Gary Nash, who have attempted to "avoid assimilation and find a genuine third way between it and separatist nationalism" and have done so by "offer[ing] a substitute for cultural parity—cultural interaction." "This is fine in itself," they write, "but it says nothing about the conditions, equal or unequal or some combination, under which interaction takes place" (89–92).[2] While I do try throughout my chapters to highlight the more painful or difficult (and even violent or tragic) aspects of the individuals' and communities' experiences, it is certainly true that both my concept of cross-cultural transformation and (especially) my focus on personal narratives and thus individual lives and perspectives do not allow for a great deal of emphasis on larger power dynamics that might be in play across or between the communities in question. Such dynamics have been, I believe, thoroughly and effectively covered in many of the best and most prominent works of multicultural American history: Howard Zinn's *A People's History of the United States* (1980) represents a broad example of that emphasis, while Francis Jennings's *The Invasion of America: Indians, Colonialism, and the Cant of Conquest* (1975) provides a more specific illustration. I would situate my project not in opposition to that emphasis, but as both a complement to it (highlighting some of the cross-cultural currents that have operated beside, or perhaps at times beneath, the more oppositional relationships) and, in its ideal form, a way to imagine an America that can move beyond hierarchies of power and privilege by defining and embracing a community in which the lines between cultures have never been fixed or absolute. As with every element of the multicultural narrative (and the traditional one as well), I envision my definition as less an absolute alternative than an addition to our sense of American history and identity, if one that I do believe has the potential to unify those seemingly contrasting accounts.

Even scholars who are perfectly willing to allow for that addition, however, might well advance the second anticipated critique: that the figures on whom my chapters focus represent special or at least unusual situations and circumstances, experiences that differentiate them from even the majority of members of their initial cultures (much less other Americans outside of those cultures). Most Spanish explorers were not separated from their expeditions and stranded in the New World for nearly a decade (as was de Vaca); most Puritan settlers were not taken captive by warring Native Americans and transported into the heart of native communities

(as was Rowlandson); most African slaves did not have the opportunity to travel extensively on naval and commercial voyages, to buy
their own freedom, and to end their lives working as abolitionists in
London (as did Equiano); and so on. I try to address this critique
directly in each chapter's opening pages, where I analyze texts produced by more "typical" members of the cultures and communities
in question, in order to make the case that cross-cultural transformation is at least hinted at in those texts as well; I return to those
broader arguments about shared experiences throughout the chapters, and particularly in their closing paragraphs. There is no question that each of my focal individuals went through noteworthy and
interesting experiences—after all, such experiences are, to a significant degree, a prerequisite for an individual's writing and publica-
tion of (or at least the success of and enduring attention to) his or
her personal narrative. Yet I would contend of all my focal figures
what I write of de Vaca in the opening of Chapter 1: his noteworthy
experiences only highlighted and perhaps exacerbated—and then
certainly provided the rationale for a personal narrative about—
cross-cultural encounters and shifts that were happening throughout the era, that were in fact the defining element of (in that case)
the process of exploration. Such encounters were of course not the
only possibility within this era, and the more overtly divisive and
violent alternatives of conquest and enslavement and destruction
have for good reason been paramount in the period's contemporary
chronicles and subsequent histories. But I would, once again, argue
both that the divisive encounters have been effectively documented
and that attention to the often more subtle but just as foundational
cross-cultural encounters allows for a new and potentially more
communal and progressive vision of American history and identity.

The third critique might come less from within the disciplines
of American studies (although this trend has certainly been a part
of recent Americanist scholarship) and more from comparative
scholars, to whom my argument might sound very much like a new
but not substantively distinct version of American exceptional-
ism. While I am not a scholar of the history or culture of any other
nation, I can certainly imagine how cross-cultural transformations
might be hugely significant to a number of other countries, especially those with large immigrant populations or multiple ethnic

or racial communities living within their borders. I would thus be entirely open to extension of my argument to such nations, with any or all of the specific distinctions and contexts that might apply; in fact my own first and fifth chapters do define "America" in at least partly hemispheric terms, including Latin America (and particularly Mexico, first in its own exploration period and then at the end of the twentieth century) in the mix as well.[3] Similarly, many of Equiano's most cross-cultural experiences and transformations take place on board the ships—whether slave, merchant, or naval vessels—that play such a prominent role in his life and identity, and there too "America" provides a gateway into a set of transnational settings and experiences. Yet I would also contend that in almost every other case, cross-cultural transformation has become a part of nations at a relatively late point in their history—such as the mid- to late twentieth and early twenty-first centuries, when worldwide migrations and communal movements and shifts have become dominant forces around the globe. In contrast, it is my argument that America has been centrally defined by such transformation from its first communal points of origin,[4] and that every century of the nation's existence (both before and after its political founding in the late eighteenth century) has similarly included cross-cultural transformations in foundational roles. And that originating and consistent place for such transformations does, I believe, distinguish America, and thus constitutes our national identity in its most unique and salient sense.

That definition and argument is, again, in conversation with a number of other scholarly perspectives from the last few decades. A particularly prominent early (and continuing) literary critical voice in that conversation is that of Werner Sollors, who in his essay "A Critique of Pure Pluralism" (1986) argues that "taken exclusively, what is often called 'the ethnic perspective'—which often means, in literary history, the emphasis of a writer's *descent*—all but annihilates polyethnic art movements, moments of individual and cultural interaction, and the pervasiveness of cultural syncretism in America" (256). Sollors advocates instead for those scholars who are both working from and analyzing "a transethnic perspective" (276–77), and in the same year modeled that work at length in his *Beyond Ethnicity: Consent and Descent in American Culture* (1986). As that book's subtitle suggests, Sollors's alternative to the ethnic perspective emphasizes consent, and specifically "look[ing] at the writings of and about people who were descended from diverse backgrounds but were, or consented to become, Americans" (7). Building directly on Sollors's emphasis on consent but expanding from literary criticism to philosophy and cultural studies is David Hollinger's *Postethnic America: Beyond Multiculturalism* (1995), in which Hollinger argues that "multiculturalism . . . has helped us to recognize and appreciate cultural diversity, but has too often left the impression that culture follows the lines of shape and color" (x). Hollinger advances as his alternative "a postethnic perspective [which] favors voluntary over involuntary affiliations, balances an appreciation for communities of descent with a determination to make room for new communities, and promotes solidarities of wide scope that incorporate people with different ethnic and racial backgrounds" (2–3). Both men link their projects explicitly to attempts to define America itself: Sollors cites Tocqueville for his most fundamental underlying question, "How can consent (and consensus) be achieved in a country whose citizens are of such heterogeneous descent?" (6) and Hollinger notes that "a postethnic perspective on American nationality emphasizes the civic character of the American nation-state, in contrast to the ethnic character of most of the nationalism we read about today" (14).

There is no question that Sollors's consensual identities and Hollinger's postethnic ones parallel my cross-cultural transformations on multiple levels, and my project is indebted to and in direct conversation with their voices and ideas. For example, Hollinger's preference for cosmopolitanism instead of pluralism, because "pluralism respects inherited boundaries and locates individuals within one or another of a series of ethno-racial groups to be protected and preserved," while "cosmopolitanism promotes multiple identities, emphasizes the dynamic and changing character of many groups, and is responsive to the potential for creating new cultural combinations" (3–4), nicely illustrates many of my objections to the multicultural narrative of American identity. Sollors's *Neither Black nor White yet Both: Thematic Explorations of Interracial Literature* (1997) represents a literary critical project that likewise parallels my close readings of cross-cultural personal narratives. Yet I would argue that both Sollors and Hollinger emphasize choice much more fully than would I, and that in doing so they limit the applicability of their ideas to a somewhat self-selected (and in some ways historically recent) community of Americans. That is, in both scholars' arguments there is a sense that certain Americans have made these choices and created new identities while others have not; and, concurrently, a sense that it is significantly easier and thus more likely for such choices to be made in the late twentieth century than at any other point in American history. I would agree with the second point, and that is one reason why emphasizing cross-cultural transformations instead—which are in many cases, including those of at least four of my five individuals, not the product of voluntary choice so much as the result of and response to experiences and encounters—can more fully extend the definition back to the multiple centuries of American history. Similarly, I believe that cross-cultural transformations are part of every individual American's and American community's experiences; sometimes those Americans are predisposed to consent to such an identity (as is certainly the case for Gloria Anzaldúa and as is, again, more possible and more likely in our present historical moment), but in any and every case they confront, are changed in one way or another by, and move through such transformations into their resulting American identities.

Just as Sollors extends his alternative definition to mixed-race lives and texts in *Neither Black nor White*, so too have many recent scholars analyzed racial mixture and hybridity in order to advance a narrative that is neither traditional nor multicultural. Exemplifying such emphases are Mary Waters's "Multiple Ethnic Identity Choices" in the collection *Beyond Pluralism: The Conception of Groups and Group Identities in America* (1998); Teresa Hubel and Neil Brooks's collection *Literature and Racial Ambiguity* (2002), the essays in which analyze "those individuals and collectives that cannot be easily categorized" (i); SanSan Kwan and Kenneth Speirs's collection *Mixing It Up: Multiracial Subjects* (2004), "the origins of [which] are rooted in [their] imaginings of the future for people of mixed race" (1); and the collections *The Politics of Multiracialism: Challenging Racial Thinking* (Dalmage, 2004) and *Identity Politics Reconsidered* (Alcoff et al. 2006). In a slightly different but definitely connected vein, Doris Sommer has advanced the literary and cultural study of bilingualism, in both her edited collection *Bilingual Games: Some Literary Investigations* (2003) and her own *Bilingual Aesthetics: A New Sentimental Education* (2004). Sommer's argument, in the latter text's introduction, that "most people live in, or at least alongside, more than one language, [which] makes switching codes (cultures, perspectives) common" (xxv), indicates how well the individuals and texts on which such projects focus can be linked to my idea of cross-cultural transformation; bilingualism in particular is critical to the transformations experienced by and represented in the narratives of all five of my individuals. Yet at the same time, most of these projects are especially concerned with individuals who are born and/or raised from birth in the categories "mixed race" or "bilingual," and such individuals are more the products of, rather than themselves experiencing, the kinds of cross-cultural transformations for which I am arguing. I analyze the identity and personal narrative of precisely such an individual, Barack Obama, in my conclusion. But if we focus only on such individuals, it might contribute to a sense that most other Americans (who are not mixed-race, who grow up speaking only one language, and so on) are less hybrid or cross-cultural; and I want to argue that Obama's hybridity, his status as a descendent of two cross-cultural transformations (about which he writes at length in that narrative), represents all of our shared American heritage and the legacy of the defining experiences illustrated by my five main figures and texts.

Finally, there have in recent years been published a number of scholarly projects that can be connected to my own even more explicitly; while each deserves to be read and responded to in full, I will here, in the spirit of the kinds of encounters and dialogues on which my definition's ideal enactment and extension depends, briefly highlight, in no particular order, a few exemplary such texts (in addition to the scholars and texts cited in each chapter's opening pages):

- David Goldstein and Aubrey Thacker's collection *Complicating Constructions: Race, Ethnicity, and Hybridity in American Texts* (2007), which operates from the aforementioned idea that "diversity within categories far exceeds diversity between categories" (xvi) and provides a variety of literary critical analyses of such complex diversity

- David Buisseret and Steven G. Reinhardt's collection *Creolization in the Americas* (2000), which (in conversation with Edouard Glissant, regarding whom see note 3) proposes the concept of creolization "to establish a theoretical framework for the syncretic process by which, as all would acknowledge, a truly New World came into being in those regions that the sixteenth-century Europeans prematurely called their 'New World'" (3)
- Sollors's collection *Multilingual America: Transnationalism, Ethnicity, and the Languages of American Literature* (1998), and especially his introductory essay "After the Culture Wars; or, From 'English Only' to 'English Plus'" (1–13)
- Lawrence Rosenwald's *Multilingual America: Language and the Making of American Literature* (2008), which "is focused on literature that seeks to represent *collective* encounters" (x) and begins the move in its concluding chapter "Towards a History of Multilingual American Literature" (146–59)
- Gerald Graff's *Beyond the Culture Wars: How Teaching the Conflicts Can Revitalize American Education* (1992), which notes that "antagonistic as they are in most respects, the liberal pluralist and the conservative solutions are actually two sides of the same coin; neither is able to imagine any positive role for cultural conflict" and argues instead for "teaching [different cultures and values] in relationship to one another so that the differences and points of intersection become comprehensible" (10, 14–15)
- Laurie Grobman's *Multicultural Hybridity: Transforming American Literary Scholarship and Pedagogy* (2007), which uses the theories of Iris Marion Young and Homi Bhabha to argue for "a U.S. literature hybridity model, . . . a theory of the hybridity of multicultural literature [which] provides the tools we need to resee *all* of American literature as an intercultural, interconnected nexus" (xiv) and "posits the whole of U.S. literature—that is, all literature written by residents of the United States—as a multidimensional, cross-cultural, and transnational formation" (L

All of these projects share a strong sense not only of the foundational quality of such mixture in American history, literature, culture, and identity, but also of both the conflicts and the opportunities that the mixtures present for those individuals and communities who experience them and for the nation that has been constituted out of them.

To analyze such individual and communal experiences across the five centuries of postcontact American existence, I turn in my chapters to extended readings of personal narratives. While my reasons for doing so are, first and foremost, practical—I cannot imagine a better place to find and analyze both the lives of exemplary Americans and how those figures imagine and represent their experiences—the genre of autobiography itself is, as I intimated above, particularly well suited for an argument about transformative identities. For one thing, the genre is itself hybrid on multiple levels, as Harold Rosen traces in his *Speaking From Memory: A Guide to Autobiographical Acts and Practices* (1998): written personal narratives tend to blur the lines between orality and textuality, and thus "autobiography becomes a classic instance of a kind of transgression" of such traditionally accepted but porous borders as those between author and reader, past and present, and reality and artistry (7); because of both those transgressions and the genre's seeming lack of creative or formal sophistication, autobiography had in scholarly circles "for a long time been marginalized as a mongrel foraging around the edge of literature. 'Hybrid' was the polite word often used" (3).[6] Moreover, autobiographies often likewise render porous and hybrid the seemingly clear barriers between individual and communal perspectives and identities, as Deborah Reed-Danahay notes in the introduction to her collection *Auto/ Ethnography: Rewriting the Self and the Social* (1997). Writing of that titular genre, she admits that "the term has a double self—referring either to the ethnography of one's own group or to autobiographical writing that has ethnographic interest"; and she connects that multigeneric nature to the writer and subject's own hybrid identity, arguing that "one of the main characteristics of an autoethnographic perspective is that the autoethnographer is a boundary-crosser, and the role can be characterized as that of a dual identity" (2–3). To my mind, every autobiographer—or at least each of my authors, although here too I believe they are representative—is an autoethnographer in these terms, portraying not only his or her individual life but also the communities within which that life has unfolded. In its generic and perspectival hybridity, then, the personal narrative constitutes as well as contains the kinds of transformations on which my argument focuses.

Moreover, there are specifically historical and national components to the genre—as illustrated by, but not unique to, my particular texts—that likewise match my project's aims. William Spengemann, one of the genre's earliest and most prominent scholars, defines in his *The Forms of Autobiography: Episodes in the History of a Literary Genre* (1980) three subgenres as they have developed over more than two millennia: historical, philosophical, and poetic autobiographies. While all three categories could be applied to my texts in certain ways, I believe that they fall most clearly into the historical subgenre, which Spengemann defines primarily through the connection of the narrator to the life being narrated: he traces the advent of historical autobiography to "the relocation of the source of the narrator's knowledge about the protagonist's life from somewhere outside that life to the life itself, and the concomitant relocation of the narrator, from a timeless ground above the protagonist's life to a point further along in the time of that life"; elaborates further that for such an author, "his narrator and protagonist are essentially the same person at different stages of enlightenment, which is to say at different points in time" (34–35); and notes the effects of this link on textual structure, since "for any historical autobiographer who makes his present knowledge the effect of causally connected experiences in his past, each event is a link in the chain that binds past to present" (37–38). In other words, the historical autobiographer's subject is precisely the life experiences that have led to his or her identity and perspective in the present—a point that, while perhaps superficially obvious, has a profound meaning in the cases of my texts and lives: whatever the exact nature or duration of the cross-cultural transformations that each individual has experienced, his or her choice to highlight and examine those transformations in the personal narrative makes clear how influential they have been in constituting the author's present self and perspective.

I want to argue that those past and present selves are not only individually and communally but also nationally illustrative, and here too American autobiography is a particularly salient genre through which to develop such an argument. Steven Hunsaker analyzes the connections of autobiography to nation in his *Autobiography and National Identity in the Americas* (1999), a book founded upon the premise that the central question for American autobiographers is "Who am I, and what role does nation play in shaping my identity?" (1). As that quote implies, Hunsaker at times constructs an explicitly hierarchical relationship and power dynamic between individual and national identities as represented in such texts, arguing for example that "for these autobiographers and for us as their readers, reliance on 'inevitable' forms of national identity leads to an understanding of the nation as an entity independent of—and thus imposed on—those who compose it rather than as their creation" (5). But he also recognizes the existence in this hybrid genre of alternative, more cross-cultural relationships, the possibility that these autobiographers can portray and embody opportunities for "forming, joining, or modifying such an inclusive nation" (3). And in his book's concluding lines he explicitly highlights both the promise and the difficulties of the latter processes, claiming that "the nine autobiographical narratives considered here illustrate both the liberating potential of seeing the nation as the product of its citizens and the instability that follows the creation and stretching of the boundaries of the imagined community" (132). That combination of liberation and instability is at the heart of both cross-cultural transformation itself and an argument that would redefine the partly imagined but unquestionably meaningful community of "America" as centrally connected to such transformations.

That argument is, ultimately, as much about the readers of my personal narratives and what they take away from those texts as it is about the identities of the books' authors and subjects, and on that point as well, autobiography is particularly suited to my purposes. As Spengemann notes of historical autobiographies, using the most famous American autobiography (Benjamin Franklin's) as his illustration, they tend to have an explicitly "public, didactic function": "the public purpose of conveying the lessons of individual experience to men who might not otherwise know them" (52). Sidonie

Smith and Julia Watson, in the introduction to their *Reading Autobi-*
ography: A Guide for Interpreting Life Narratives (2001), extend and
amplify that point on two levels: noting how much autobiography
can reveal about a shared past, since "in the details and the immedi-
acy of the lived lives of such autobiographical narrators, the political
and cultural contexts of the historical past become vivid and memo-
rable" (11); but making clear the complex, hybrid process by which
that past is created, since "autobiographical truth is a different matter: it is an intersubjective exchange between narrator and reader
aimed at producing a shared understanding of the meaning of a life"
(13). What Smith and Watson term the "intersectional identities"
(36–37) at the core of autobiographical writing thus comprise inter-
sections not only between the author's past and present selves, individual and communal identities, and real and artistic perspectives
(among other dualities) but also (and just as importantly) between
author and readers, constituting a final, paramount, and ongoing
cross-cultural transformation that can be experienced by all who
encounter and engage with these personal narratives.

In the chapters that follow, I encounter and engage with six such
narratives, with an immediate goal of transforming our perspective
on American history, culture, and identity in each of the moments
and centuries from which that narrative and figure emerged. But my
ultimate aim is more ambitious still: to alter our national definition,
to provide in cross-cultural transformation an alternative to the
traditional and multicultural narratives that can bridge the opposition between those perspectives, transcend the images of relatively
distinct and static cultures on which both narratives depend, and
envision an America that is instead centrally defined by the dynamic
process through which individuals and communities shift from their
cultural starting points into something much more hybrid, evolving, difficult, and potentially transformative in the most productive
and ideal senses. Certainly such a shift would affect many of the
specific debates and controversies that have constituted the culture
wars, and with which I began this introduction. But more broadly
and critically, a definition of American identity as cross-cultural
transformation would give new and more vital meaning to some
of our nation's most accepted and yet divisive tropes: clichéd but
ubiquitous phrases like "All-American," "American values," and "real

Americans." As I argue in the conclusion, the ways in which Barack Obama has been and continues to be both subtly and overtly defined as outside such concepts indicates how influential they remain to our national definitions, and how significant such a redefinition can thus be. That is, if we see Obama as the complex, hybrid heir to a heritage of cross-cultural transformations—and moreover and more importantly still, see that heritage as the core of American history and identity throughout the centuries, and thus Obama's status as profoundly representative of where we're all coming from—then it allows us to imagine a future in which we build upon that shared identity and produce an American community that lives up to and extends the legacy of all the cross-cultural transformations that have shaped our nation. Grobman notes in her book's final chapter that a vision of American literature as fundamentally hybrid depends on "a journey not only into the future, but into the past, and one that must occur multi-directionally and cross-culturally" (148). It is my sincere hope that this book can, through my analyses of the cross-cultural transformations that have defined American history and identity, help highlight and analyze some exemplary milestones along that journey, and so help move us a bit closer toward what Obama has rightfully envisioned as the embodiment of "A More Perfect Union."

I

Transformative Explorations

Cabeza de Vaca Changes His Skin

Christopher Columbus's famous letter to Luis de Santangel, written in February 1493 at the height of his first voyage's promise, exemplifies how fully both the perspective and experience of exploration seem to depend on distinct, opposed, and hierarchical cultural identities. When Columbus, writing to this member of the Spanish court for the express purpose of "pleas[ing]" him with "the great victory with which Our Lord has crowned [the] voyage," engages at all with the native cultures here, it is only to dismiss entirely, usually within the same sentence, their existence outside of a European framework: he notes for example that the islands are "filled with people innumerable" and then in the next clause claims that "of them all I have taken possession for their highnesses," and the fact that "them" could refer either to the islands or to the people is precisely the point, as both are simply material for Spanish conquest. And certainly the islands are the more significant material, as clarified in the second such sentence: "[My men] traveled three days' journey and found an infinity of small hamlets and people without number, but nothing of importance." So unimportant are the native cultures, in fact, that Columbus can acknowledge the native name for the first island, "Guanahani," while noting without the slightest hesitation that he gave to "each one [of the islands] a new name" in Spanish. Having thus fully established that the native cultures exist simply as potential fodder for, and more likely minor obstacles on, the path to the European cultures' conquests, Columbus turns in the long subsequent paragraph to his famous descriptions of this marvelous new world, which entirely elide the innumerable natives in favor of the "thousand kinds" of trees and birds and fruits (11–12). There is literally no place for these other cultures in the shared cultural perspective of explorer and audience.

Exploration was only the first step in the European cultures' encounters with the New World and its native cultures, however, and in the case of Columbus, subsequent texts reveal that the Santangel letter's clear cultural divisions did not entirely survive later encounters. More exactly, Columbus's letter to Ferdinand and Isabella, written a decade later on the occasion of his catastrophic fourth voyage, highlights two subtle but important shifts in the explorer's perspective on the place and cultures over those ten years. The letter's ostensible purpose and most of its content are entirely self-interested and self-serving: Columbus has been stripped by rivals of much of his royally invested power and imprisoned, and is writing to seek redress for those wrongs and reclamation of the rewards for his years of service to the Crown. Yet within his complaints and self-justifications lie two more complex transformations in his visions of the New World and his relationship to it. Where the first letter had focused entirely on the land's possibilities for European conquest, now Columbus complains that his many rival explorers "go forth to plunder," and that in so doing they not only "prejudice [his] honor" but also "do very great damage to the enterprise." The opposite of plunder is not necessarily respectful preservation, but there is a sense here that Columbus's vision of the enterprise has begun to diverge from that of many of his fellow European explorers, perhaps in part because he has lost the authority to claim and rename what he encounters. More explicitly reflecting those personal transformations is his final and most surprising complaint: "Here in the Indies I have become careless of the prescribed forms of religion." For most of the letter it is the changed circumstances on which Columbus has dwelled, but here he makes clear that his own identity and perspective have likewise been changed by his time in the New World; the changes are of course far from positive, and in fact he argues that his "soul will be forgotten if it here leaves [his] body," but they nonetheless illustrate the transformative power of a decade in contact with the New World and its "million savages," those other cultures now both quantifiable and clearly important to the explorer's experiences (13–14).

As Rex Nettleford argues in the afterword to his coedited collection *Race, Discourse, and the Origins of the Americas* (1995), a genuinely cross-cultural understanding of the exploration era can shift our perspective on not only the roles of and interactions between European and native cultures but also the era's most mythical (and most vilified) figures, allowing Columbus and his cohort to become part of a new narrative about "the development of a creolized civilization" in the Americas (287).[1] But while examining Columbus's multiple stages of experience can thus help undermine any absolute divisions between the explorers' cultures and those that they encountered in the New World, it is another Spanish explorer, Alvar Nuñez Cabeza de Vaca, whose experiences most fully exemplify the cross-cultural transformations at the heart of the exploration process. The obviously extreme nature of de Vaca's[2] time in the New World—after the expedition on which he served as an officer was shipwrecked on Florida's Gulf Coast, he spent the next nine years making his way across the continent in the company of various native tribes and cultures—rather than distinguishing him from the typical European explorer, provides instead a particularly strong lens through which the cross-cultural transformations that always accompanied exploration can be perceived and analyzed. That is, de Vaca's nine years in America forced him to confront the meanings of encounter, of a European perspective and identity affecting and being affected by those of Native Americans, in a way that was simply more explicit than the subtle processes at work throughout the exploration period.

The biographical and anthropological investigations into de Vaca's journey and world by scholars such as David Howard (1997) and Alex Krieger (2002) have provided a strong contextual foundation for such ideas about his representative qualities. On a more philosophical level, my reading of de Vaca is in conversation with Harold Augenbraum and Margarita Fernández Olmos, who choose to begin their *Latino Reader* with de Vaca and define him, in his status as "a cultural hybrid created by the American experience," as "a symbolic precursor of the Chicano/a" (xv). Certainly it is possible to define de Vaca as, instead, a more subtle but just as potent conquistador; Lázaro Lima, in a recent critique of scholars such as Augenbraum and Olmos, reads de Vaca's journey as "a trope for the strategic incorporation (assimilation) and eventual digestion (consumption) of Amerindian culture through the printed word" (102). But despite de Vaca's eventual (if partial) return to a Spanish and European identity and perspective, his experiences in the New World illustrate how much such cultural identities were altered by, while themselves impacting and likewise reshaping, the identities and cultures they encountered. Moreover, de Vaca provides, in his extended personal narrative of his experiences, a text that, in its form as well as its themes, allows his audiences—whether contemporary and European or twenty-first century and American—to engage with and analyze his transformative explorations.

It is in fact with an explicit and extended address to his most direct audience, the Spanish King and Holy Roman Emperor Charles V, that de Vaca begins his narrative. Unsurprisingly, de Vaca focuses much of this letter on the question of service; not only is he writing to his culture's highest worldly authority, but de Vaca had served as an officer in the Spanish fleet, making service to Charles a defining aspect of his identity on multiple levels. Yet he frames that service, and thus that identity, in two complex ways that serve to divide him from his monarch as much as connect the two figures. On a general level, de Vaca makes the rather strange observation that "we see not only countrymen, whom faith and duty oblige to do this, but even foreigners striv[ing] to exceed their efforts" in service to Charles. Both the sentence's pronoun use, the relatively objective "we" and the lack of a possessive "our" before "countrymen," and the somewhat dismissive "oblige to do this" seem to place de Vaca at a remove from Charles and his national servants, to define the narrator as something other than the Spanish officer he had been a decade before.[3] Such a remove would not, the sentence makes clear, render him less dutiful to the monarch; but this point too de Vaca complicates, arguing in the next sentences that "there is a very great disparity" in service caused "by fortune," and that one who has suffered at fortune's hands "cannot demonstrate any greater witness to his intention than his diligence, and even this is sometimes so obscured that it cannot make itself evident." (45–46). The straightforward identity of a Spanish naval officer has, only a few lines into the letter, already been transformed into something at least partially foreign and obscured, distinct from the clear cultural and social roles to which it would generally be connected.

Interestingly, de Vaca seems painfully aware of those transformations, and in the letter's final line explicitly links them to his experiences in the New World, asking that his text "be received in the name of service, because this alone is what a man who came away naked could carry out with him." He thus introduces his narrative as serving a somewhat contradictory double role: on the one hand it is an explicit reminder of all that he lost over his near-decade of wandering (not only his clothes but, it would seem, much of the cultural identity and role that they signified); yet on the other it can become an act of service that reconnects him to his monarch and culture. And in fact de Vaca links those two meanings of his narrative into one complex chain, arguing that he "had no opportunity to perform greater service than this, which is to bring to [Charles] an account of all that I was able to observe and learn in the nine years that I walked lost and naked through many and very strange lands." That is, the loss of all accoutrements of identity prompted the narrative's alternative service; as de Vaca puts it in the next sentence, "because although the hope that I had of coming out from among them was always very little, my care and effort to remember everything in detail was always very great." The awkwardness of "because although," far from a simple gap in translation (de Vaca writes *"porque aun que,"* placing the two conjunctions in this awkward sequence), reveals the causal link yet also the distinction between these two stages in de Vaca's exploration experience: the years among distinct cultures in the New World and their attendant identity transformations; and the production of the narrative, which will both capture those changes and attempt to reconcile them with de Vaca's foundational identity and culture (46–47).

The first quarter of de Vaca's narrative reveals few signs of these complexities or transformations, however. As an officer on the expedition, de Vaca was in the service of not only Charles V but also his most direct representative, the expedition's governor (leader) Pánfilo de Narváez; certain of his roles are thus explicitly communal, both in the past (to follow the governor's orders) and in the present (to narrate the expedition's group experiences more than his own individual ones). Typical of both roles is the following passage: "And the next day the governor decided to go inland to explore the land and see what it contained. The commissary, the inspector of mines, and I went with him, with forty men, and among them six horsemen, whose horses were of little use to us. We followed to the north until, at the hour of vespers, we arrived at a very large bay that seemed to us to go far inland" (55). Not only is the governor the moment's principal subject, but also de Vaca locates himself as only one (and not even the first or second) of those who follow his lead; the structure of the second sentence, with its multiple subordinate clauses modifying the "forty men," lessens even that presence, so that the "I" almost entirely vanishes into the communal action. Even the perception of the land with which the quoted section concludes is a communal one. And later, when the expedition has begun to encounter the grave difficulties that will eventually divide it irrevocably, de Vaca's narration makes clear the stakes in maintaining this communal identity and role: he concludes a section where the healthier men (including himself) have opted to remain with the sicker ones (including the governor) by noting that they have "affirm[ed] that what would be the fate of one would be the fate of all without any one abandoning the others" (71).

The expedition's identity is not just communal, of course, but is specifically European and conquest driven, and those aspects are likewise prominent in de Vaca's narrative throughout this opening section. De Vaca does have his own voice and perspective, elided as they may be for much of this portion of his text, and they come through clearly when the governor formally asks for his opinion on a particular course of action: de Vaca disagrees strenuously with the governor's plans, and spends more than thirty lines narrating his contrasting opinion. But when the governor insists on continuing with his own plans and indicates that de Vaca can remain behind, so as not to require him to pursue a path with which he disagrees, de Vaca demands instead to accompany the governor, and his reasons for doing so seem clearly connected to the European culture of conquest of which he is a part. He wants to make it known (both to the governor and to his audience), for example, that he is "more willing than he and the others . . . to expose myself to danger and endure whatever he and the others [are] to endure than to take charge of the ships and give occasion that it be said . . . that I remained out of fear, for which my honor would be under attack." In fact, he admits, he "prefer[s] risking my life to placing my honor in jeopardy" (58–59). Such sentiments, expressed as they may be in opposition to the expedition's leader, would likely be seconded by most of de Vaca's fellow officers and soldiers; reputation and honor, as his narrative and so many others (including Columbus's 1503 letter) make plain, were central to the perspectives of the era's explorers.

Equally central to those perspectives were the opposed and hierarchical visions of native cultures exemplified by Columbus's 1493 letter, and de Vaca's opening section likewise falls in line with that cultural viewpoint. His genre allows him to describe the expedition's encounters with natives at much greater length than Columbus did, but the first few such encounters define those natives as entirely distinct from, hostile to, and fodder for the explorers' culture and goals. The first encounter, for example, ostensibly highlights only the gap between the cultures—de Vaca notes that "although they spoke to us, since we did not have an interpreter we did not understand them"—but intimates a perceived hostility ("they made many signs and threatening gestures to us and it seemed to us that they were telling us to leave the land") that would justify an equally hostile, conquering response (54–55). Later, when hostilities become more overt, de Vaca narrates them as an explicit clash of cultures: "They shot at one of our Christians, and God willed that they not wound him" (63). Despite these conflicts, and unlike Columbus, de Vaca is certainly interested in observing and describing these distinct cultures, but he does so throughout this opening section through the explicit lens of a would-be conqueror: his first extended description of the native people focuses almost exclusively on their abilities as archers and the "great strength and agility" with which they wield their impressive bows (68); and after his first experience with native religious customs he immediately dismisses them as "a type of idolatry," followed by four sentences in which he interrogates those natives about where they found the "samples of gold" used in the ceremonies (56). The divisions between the native and explorers' cultures seem clear and absolute throughout this opening section, within de Vaca's perspective just as much as in that of the expedition overall.

Yet at two moments in the narrative's opening pages, that overall cultural identity is revealed to be less stable or fixed than it might seem, and de Vaca's inclusion and framing of these moments foreshadows his own subsequent transformations. Significantly, he chooses to begin his narrative of the expedition's experiences in the New World with the first such moment: after a few sentences describing the expedition's composition and departure from Spain, he writes, "We arrived at the island of Santo Domingo, where we spent nearly forty-five days stocking up on certain necessary items, notably horses. Here more than one hundred and forty men of our crew deserted us, choosing to remain there because of the favors and promises that the men of that land made to them" (48). The communal pronoun use, and thus the differentiation of de Vaca's culture from both "the men of that land" and these deserters, is prominent here, but so too is the fact, highlighted by de Vaca's use of specifics, that within the first six weeks in the New World almost a quarter of the expedition's six hundred men have been sufficiently influenced as to abandon that community in favor of the new one. More singular and complex, and even more relevant to de Vaca's later experiences, is the second desertion, one that follows closely upon the expression of communal solidarity quoted above; the expedition is bartering with a group of natives for much-needed supplies, and de Vaca notes that "a Greek Christian named Doreteo Teodoro . . . said that he wanted to go with [the natives]. The governor and others tried very hard to prevent him from going, but they were unable, since in any case he wanted to go with them. And so he left, and took a black man with him" (78). On the one hand these two deserters are explicitly identified as already distinct (in nationality or race) from the Spanish explorers' culture; but on the other Teodoro and his choice echo de Vaca's opening reference to foreign service to Charles V, highlighting how such national roles and cultural unity can be (in that letter's terms) obscured and transformed amid—and because of—the New World experiences and cultures.

There is, it is important to note, no indication in this passage that de Vaca is ready to make such a choice and abandon his role and culture. But it is only a few days later that he is forced to do so, in a moment that he narrates in such a way as to make the transition from a communal to an individual identity as clear as possible. Presented with multiple forward paths, de Vaca turns (this time with no hesitation or disagreement) to the governor, admitting that the men "had to be able to follow him and do what he had commanded," and thus that "he should tell me what it was that he ordered me to do." But Narváez shatters that military and cultural chain of command, answering de Vaca that "it was no longer time for one man to rule another, that each one should do whatever seemed best to him in order to save his own life, and that he intended so to do it. And saying this he veer[s] away with his raft. And since [de Vaca is] unable to follow him, [he] head[s] for the other raft that was at sea, which waited for" him (81–82). Despite the very literal meaning of "unable to follow him," this also marks the first time in the narrative when de Vaca has no clear orders, no explicit officer's role to play; even when he had disagreed with his orders and pursued his own honor, it was explicitly within the framework of his communal and cultural identity. Now that identity has veered away from de Vaca, and he is left with no option but to shift from the communal to the individual, to save his own life. But there is, as of this moment in the narrative, a very real question as to whether that individual identity comprises much more than an empty shell, a circumstance symbolized by de Vaca's description of himself and the few men who survive the subsequent wreckage of his raft: "naked as the day we were born" and having "lost everything we carried with us. And although all of it was of little value, at that time it was worth a great deal" (85–86).

One could, with a good deal of accuracy, describe the next eight years of de Vaca's life—and the remaining half of his narrative—as an attempt to reclaim the things he carried, to find his cultural identity once more. In the process, however, he will journey to an interconnected but shifting series of places, both geographic and within his identity and perspective, that influence and transform him in profound and, I would argue, permanent ways. Those transformations have in fact already begun, in a small but important way, in his first encounter with natives after the expedition's division. De Vaca hears from a scout that the land bears signs of cultivation and livestock, leading to their shared but erroneous culturally-based perception that "for this reason it must be land inhabited by Christians." When they encounter the local, decidedly non-Christian natives, the Spanish are no longer in a position to treat them as potentially hostile but must instead, "as best" they can, "try to assure them and reassure ourselves" of their peaceful intentions; perhaps because of this attitude of mutual assurance, the natives reply in kind, giving de Vaca an arrow, "which is a sign of friendship," and "by gestures . . . [telling] us that they [will] return in the morning and bring us food to eat" (83–84). Or perhaps this drastically different reception is due to what de Vaca admits are the equally distinct "conditions in which we [find] ourselves"—that is, this nonconquering relationship with the natives cannot be separated from the distance these men have already traveled from their cultural identities. De Vaca notes that, when the natives see them "dressed so differently from the first time, and in such a strange state, they [are] so frightened that they [withdraw]" (85–86); but the fright here is due not to cultural hostility but to the explorers' transformations, and so can be alleviated with precisely the kind of concurrently transformed attitude de Vaca and his men display.

It is more accurate, though, to describe this new attitude as partially transformed, since in the subsequent, extended encounter with the natives, de Vaca vacillates widely between a European cultural perspective and a connection with this new culture on which he now depends for his survival. The natives immediately welcome de Vaca and his men into the tribe, performing a ritual weeping ceremony that is meaningful not only on an empathetic level ("they all [began] to weep loudly and so sincerely that they could be heard a great distance away") but on a cultural one as well. But de Vaca narrates his response to the ceremony as a self-absorbed and still very European one: "Truly, to see that these men, so lacking in reason and so crude in the manner of brutes, grieve so much for us, increase[s] in me and in others of my company even more the magnitude of our suffering and the estimation of our misfortune." Similarly, although de Vaca realizes that he and his men have no choice if they are to survive but to "beseech" the natives to "take us to their houses," he does so with the constant apprehension that they are about to be sacrificed "to their idols"; the night of "great celebration" that follows only heightens their concern, and in fact de Vaca describes his company as "awaiting the moment when they would sacrifice us." By the morning they are, of course, still alive, and de Vaca concludes his narration of the encounter by highlighting another partial but meaningful transformation in his cultural attitude: "In the morning they again gave us fish and roots and treated us so well that we were somewhat reassured, and we lost some of our fear of being sacrificed" (86–88).

Despite this extremely welcoming treatment, however, de Vaca has at this early stage of his individual experience taken on one central and largely negative new role: captive. His survival depends not only on provisions from the natives but also on their will and power at all times. This is made perfectly clear in a long passage that follows closely upon the aforementioned ceremonies; a number of natives (as well as many of de Vaca's men) have died from "a stomach ailment," and the natives think

> that we were the ones who had killed them. And taking this to be very true, they planned among themselves to kill those of us who remained. When they came to put it into effect, an Indian in whose possession I had been placed told them they should not believe that we were the ones who killed them, because if we had such power, we would not have allowed so many of our own to die. . . . And our Lord God granted that the others followed this advice and opinion, and thus they were diverted from their intention. (89–90)

The subject of that final sentence notwithstanding, it is the natives who are the sole actors here, and de Vaca and his company are thoroughly objects: objects of the proposed action; objects of the discussion (held only among the natives, with no referenced input from the Spanish) that prevents that action; and, in the passage's (and one of the narrative's) most significant single phrase, objects that can be "placed" in the "possession" of particular natives. While de Vaca will take on a number of other and more potentially powerful (and certainly more active) roles over the remainder of the narrative, it is important to keep in mind that this status never fully changes: he will remain a kind of captive, or at least largely dependent upon the native cultures for his food (a subject away from which the narrative will never move for long), shelter, and continuing survival, for the next eight years.

Of the many effects produced by this extreme shift in roles, perhaps the most surprising and certainly one of the most significant is its introduction of a new, ethnographic tone to the narrative. The first such ethnographic passage literally follows, in the next sentence, the near-death experience quoted above; de Vaca notes that "to this island we gave the name *Malhado*," and if both that name (which translates as "Ill Fate") and his following description of the natives' "great skill" in employing their bows and arrows seem directly related to his status as the tribe's powerless, threatened captive, that connection by no means provides a sufficient rationale for the 32 subsequent sentences of ethnographic description (90–93).

Nor can the possibility of future conquest—to which de Vaca had alluded in his letter to Charles as a benefit of his years of observations of the native cultures—explain much of this extended passage, nor the many like it which the remainder of the narrative includes. That is, there would seem to be no obvious practical reason, on either the individual or the communal level, for de Vaca to include extended and painstakingly accurate descriptions of how this tribe mourns a dead child, of their marriage and family customs, of their relatively liberated perspective on women's rights, or most of the other topics through which this ethnographic passage moves. It is of course true that de Vaca simply has more time to make and develop such observations, given that his explorer's objectives have entirely disappeared: the topic of gold does not come up in these native encounters. But it is more than just his objectives that have been transformed; his perspective as well has shifted, allowing him to look at the natives not from a culturally defined view (idolatry, brutes), but rather with the combination of accuracy and sympathy that is necessary for successful ethnographic study. Thus, accompanying that perspective shift are the first signs of an identity transformation, one that has already moved de Vaca significantly closer to the natives on whom he now depends.

That move and transformation are heightened by two additional, more powerful roles that de Vaca begins to perform in the native societies with which he now travels. The first, that of a healer, is initially forced upon de Vaca and his men, and seemingly unrelated to their specific identities: the natives try "to make us physicians [*físicos*] without examining us or asking us . . . for our titles," simply in the hopes that they will "make ourselves useful." Not surprisingly, the men respond from a European perspective, laughing and "saying that it [is] a mockery and that we [do] not know how to cure." But here again de Vaca's role as a captive directly influences his cultural perspective and identity—most obviously because the men are denied food unless they go along, and soon find themselves "in such need that we [have] to do it"; but also because de Vaca is able to have an extended conversation with a particular native, who explains at length both the typical procedure and his belief that the captives in fact have "greater virtue and capacity" than the native healers. The need for food may be the direct cause of de Vaca adopting this role, but it seems clear that the conversation is the deeper reason behind both the four-sentence description of native healing with which he interrupts the narrative here and the men's subsequent attempt to create their own, cross-cultural "manner" of "perform[ing] cures," one that combines Christian gestures with native items and that works convincingly enough to yield "restored and healthy" native patients (93–94).

De Vaca's second, more individualized role is likewise both a practical response to particular, desperate conditions and a meaningful stage in his ongoing cross-cultural identity transformation. Having remained with the same native tribe for over a year, and being dissatisfied with "the great labors they force me to perform and the bad treatment," de Vaca seeks a way to connect to other tribes, a reason for "going over to the others." He finds it in the "vocation" of "merchant," a go-between who is able to remain neutral in the "continual warfare in the land," circumvent the problem of "little traffic or communication among" the various tribes, and so "obtain the things" that each tribe needs. Interestingly, the majority of those needs, or at least those that de Vaca mentions, connect directly to his prior role as healer; he particularly highlights the "conch shells with which they cut a fruit that is like *frijoles,* with which they perform cures and do their dances and make celebrations (and this is the thing of greatest value that there is among them)." Again de Vaca has taken on a role of great importance to the tribes, has taken their spiritual customs in his hands just as literally as he had taken their lives; and again taking on that role significantly alters his relationship to the natives, giving him "the freedom to go wherever I want" and allowing him to feel "not constrained in any way nor enslaved." In fact, his cross-cultural combination of healer and merchant is such a unique identity that the same man who is still in some ways a possession has become at the same time a sought-after commodity, with those natives who do "not know me desir[ing] and endeavor[ing] to see me because of my renown" (96–98).

Paralleling these identity shifts, and also extending in both time and significance de Vaca's evolving relationships to both the Spanish and native communities, are the multiple narrator's roles that he balances in this section of the narrative. While his primary role remains that of a personal narrator, telling the story of his own life over these years, that role is now bounded by two distinct and yet somewhat overlapping communal roles: on the one hand the aforementioned role of ethnographer, describing the customs and lives of the natives with whom he travels; and on the other that of the expedition's chronicler, attempting to keep track of the experiences of all his surviving fellow explorers. Within one six-page section (chapter 18 in the later, more structured edition of de Vaca's narrative), he modulates between all three narrative roles: the chapter begins in the midst of de Vaca's third-hand but painstakingly detailed account of the captivity experiences of Hernando de Esquivel, another survivor; a particular detail of Esquivel and his men's treatment leads de Vaca to "a custom [the natives] have" and "the reason they do this," the discussion of which segues into a much longer ethnographic description of the natives in question; and that description comes back around, as his narrative so often does, to details of food, which leads de Vaca to remember that "many times when we were with these people, we went three or four days without eating," and he thus resumes his own narrative for the chapter's final two pages (104–10). This constant shifting in the narrator's role not only complicates the narrative's identity at the same moment that de Vaca's own identity is adding so many roles and layers but also reinforces the ways in which his individual experiences are now both inside and outside of the native and expedition communities; he has significant ties to both cultures, and thus reasons to include details related to both, but is also more of an observer and reporter than a full participant in either.

Yet even that insider-outsider balance, intricate as it is, does not fully describe the shifts in de Vaca's communal connections over the course of this middle section of his narrative. His reports of the expedition's ongoing hardships are, as in the case with Esquivel, largely second- or third-hand, reflecting the continued connections but also the growing gaps between the explorers' experiences; whereas his ethnographic descriptions often deal with not only what he witnessed while among the tribes but also what he experienced alongside them. As he nears the food-centered conclusion of the ethnographic section in chapter 18, and transitions back to his personal narrative, there is a particularly clear example of this shared communal experience: "And in this way they satisfy their hunger two or three times a year at as great a cost as I have said. And for having lived through it, I can affirm that no hardship endured in the world equals this one" (109). The first sentence seems to differentiate between the third- and first-person pronouns, to keep in place the "their experiences" and "my narration" distinction that is crucial to ethnography, but the start of the second sentence immediately collapses that divide, making clear that de Vaca's ability to describe these peoples is directly connected to what he can "affirm" from crucial life experience. And in light of that dramatic communal connection, another, easily overlooked pronoun choice in this section, de Vaca's use of possessive pronouns to identify the men's various tribes, becomes potentially symbolic as well as practical. That is, when de Vaca writes that he and his companions "saw some Indians who were coming to see ours" (98), or later when the men are separated and he narrates the action as "each one [going] off with his Indians" (111), the pronoun usage does not simply provide a shorthand method for keeping the various tribes clear; it also highlights how de Vaca, who began his captivity as a possession in the most literal sense, now possesses a connection to the native culture that is precisely the kind of metonymic communal bond through which much of identity is constructed.

Moreover, de Vaca's ceremonial role and presence in the tribe likewise continue to evolve and deepen in this section. De Vaca and his men no longer play the role of healer out of a sense of desperation or hunger, but rather communal obligation; "some Indians" come to them and "beg us to cure them" and they oblige, without any of the reservations or argument with which the role was inaugurated (114). The role has in fact become a defining attribute of de Vaca's past and present identity within the tribe: he is subsequently approached by natives who hope that he will "cure them because they [hold him] in esteem, and they remember that [he] had cured them at the nut-gathering grounds." He does so, in the narrative's most extended description of this role, and his successes highlight the role's ceremonial and spiritual as well as its practical characteristics; the natives who seek out his healing in increasing numbers say of de Vaca and his men that they are "truly . . . children of the sun." If that identification intimates the ways in which they have begun to influence the tribe's beliefs and mythologies as well as its everyday realities, the passage immediately following it exemplifies that complex and crucial spiritual role. The natives whom de Vaca has cured tell him "something very strange," a story of a trickster figure, "a man they call an evil being [*mala cosa*]," who had passed through their land "some fifteen or sixteen years ago," done physical and psychological damage to the tribe, and then disappeared into "his house . . . below . . . a cleft in the earth." De Vaca and his men initially respond from their European cultural viewpoint, "laugh[ing] a great deal about these things" and "making fun of them," but when the natives provide proof of "the scars" that the trickster's presence has left in the tribe, the men's response becomes significantly more nuanced. It remains connected to their European culture, if in a much more sympathetic vein: the men ask the natives "to understand that, if they believe in God our Lord and [are] Christians like us, they would not be afraid of him, nor would he dare to come and do those things to them, and they could be assured that as long as we [are] in the land, he would not dare to appear in it," and the assurances work, with the natives "los[ing] a great deal of the fear they had" (116–21). Yet this is also a deeply communal moment, one quite specific to the natives' culture and identities, not only because it emphasizes the men's continuing presence with the tribe, but also because it turns the men into active participants in the tribe's developing mythology, making them into spiritual forces in a much broader and more eternal way than the powerful but temporally bound instances of healing could ever accomplish.

If the men's spiritual presence thus seems destined to remain part of the tribe, however, their actual experiences in this tribe's land are, as is the case throughout the narrative, transient. Within a page of the trickster story the men have encountered and joined another tribe's community, each man connecting with a particular native who takes him "by the hand" and "to their houses" (122). Nor will they remain in those houses for long; by far the most defining characteristic of de Vaca's experiences in the New World, after all, is movement—this is true on the largest level, as he and his men make their way across the continent from Florida to the western coast of Mexico; and on the smallest, as almost every day entails a constant, mobile search for food and other necessities. Moreover, the aforementioned continual shifts in both the narrative's focus and de Vaca's role as narrator provide an exact textual parallel to this constant movement: with each new location and tribe, de Vaca has the opportunity for further ethnographic observation and description; he learns and can report further details of the expedition's survivors and their ongoing experiences; and of course his own changing personal experiences must be recounted as well. All these movements thus constitute, paradoxically but crucially, the most stable aspect of de Vaca's New World identity; that is, while hunger is perhaps the most consistently referenced state of being in de Vaca's narrative, transformation—of place, of community, of roles—is the most prominent one. Perhaps the narrative's single most meaningful phrase, then, is a simile through which de Vaca describes the men's condition as they move away from the trickster tribe and into the next one: "throughout this entire land, we went about naked, and since we were not accustomed to it, like serpents we changed our skins twice a year" (122–23).

Central as the movements and their accompanying transformations are to de Vaca's experiences and narrative, and driven as they often are by immediate and practical concerns of hunger and survival, they are also consistently in service of a more long-range and explicitly cultural purpose: finding and reconnecting to other "Christians," other Spanish explorers or expeditions. And it is precisely this ongoing cultural goal, contrasted and yet interconnected with de Vaca's relationship to the native cultures, which provides over the final quarter of his narrative a series of complex moments that greatly influence de Vaca's experiences and identity. The first such moment also represents de Vaca's clearest recognition of these competing cultural perspectives and presences in his identity and text. As he concludes his narrative's longest ethnographic section, a four-page discussion that has focused largely on the particular tribe's preparations for and practices of war, de Vaca acknowledges his audience, implicitly but still more directly than he has for much of the narrative, noting, "This I have wanted to tell because, beyond the fact that all men desire to know the customs and practices of others, the ones who sometime might come to confront them should be informed about their customs and stratagems, which tend to be of no small advantage in such cases" (129–30). It is difficult to identify the hierarchy of these two reasons for the ethnographic description: on the one hand the strategic European motivation is "beyond" the knowledge-based, cross-cultural one, and as the predicate of the sentence is likewise privileged grammatically; but on the other the knowledge is something definite (a "fact") and universal ("all men desire"), while the strategy is uncertain ("sometime might come") and limited ("the ones"). The sentence thus reflects de Vaca's own internal divisions about the motivation for his narrative and, concurrently, his own identity vis-à-vis these two distinct and in many ways competing cultural perspectives.

It is due at least partly to those internal divisions that de Vaca begins in the following pages to consider the more negative effects of his presence among the tribes. Much of the narrative has focused on the men's positive influences, and particularly the value of their roles as healers and (in de Vaca's individual case) merchants for the tribes. But in this section de Vaca admits that those natives who are traveling with his company often "treat the others very badly," using the men's unusual presence as an excuse to shatter all rules of community and hospitality, "taking their possessions and sacking their houses without leaving them any single thing." Moreover, the men's spiritual roles are transformed in these scenarios into a justification for such communal violence: "The attackers, to console [their victims], told them that we were children of the sun, and that we had the power to cure the sick and to kill them. . . . and to be careful not to anger us in anything, and to give us everything they had, and to try to take us where there were many people, and that wherever we arrived, to steal and loot what the others had, because such was the custom" (137–39). If the trickster story exemplified how the men had contributed a positive lasting influence to the native society's beliefs, this moment makes clear that their customs have been impacted in a similar but more destructive manner. Yet it is more accurate to highlight the two influences' interconnections—de Vaca continues to heal natives throughout this section, participates in a variety of ceremonies, and even becomes a spiritual guide for those natives most directly victimized by the new destructive customs: "Those who remained dispossessed always followed us, from which the number of people grew to compensate for their loss" (143–44). If de Vaca's culture and community have been transformed through his experiences with the natives, so too, clearly, the native cultures and communities have undergone their own meaningful and lasting shifts; the ever-expanding traveling tribe surrounding and including the men seems in fact to have its own culture and identity, one certainly linked to the people who constitute it, yet also comprising a new set of customs, beliefs, and relationships.

It is, coincidentally but crucially, only after this new, hybrid culture has come into existence that de Vaca accomplishes his long-range goal and hears "news of Christians." Since this is the first time in almost a decade that he has received even slightly credible accounts of the presence of members of his own culture—I am purposefully not including the information he has learned and reported about his fellow wandering expedition members, since they have always been in situations parallel to de Vaca's and thus similarly outside of that fixed cultural identity—it stands to reason that his initial response is a joyous one, giving "many thanks to God our Lord" for what he hears. Yet that response is immediately followed by a very different and much more cross-cultural response: the men reassure their traveling tribe that they are "going to look for [the Christians] to tell them that they should not kill [the natives] or take them as slaves, nor should they take them out of their lands, nor should they do them any other harm whatsoever." De Vaca has been looking for just such a group for his entire time in the New World, but his new community now provides a very different, and even more pressing, motivation for finding them: to protect that community, to ensure its survival in the face of a potentially hostile culture. As the men hear more news of this group of Christians, those concerns are heightened, since they are told that "the Christians [have] entered the land and [have] destroyed and burned the villages and carried off half the men and all the women and boys." And this "terroriz[ing]" of the natives is destructive not simply to the communities of which the men have become so much a part, but also to the men's links to those communities; de Vaca "fear[s]" that the natives will "treat us cruelly and make us pay for what the Christians [are] doing to them" (155–57).

As has been the case throughout the narrative, de Vaca's particular identification of the group in question reflects his complex perspective on them. During his decade in the New World he has consistently identified the group for whom he is searching as "other Christians," an implicit indication of the continuing presence of his European culture, but having found them here he refers to them instead with the more neutral "the Christians." On one level this subtle difference indicates de Vaca's desire to distinguish himself from this new group, particularly in terms of how they treat the natives; he argues explicitly in the midst of this section that "it is clearly seen that all these peoples, to be drawn to become Christians and to obedience to the Imperial Majesty, must be given good treatment, and that this is the path most certain and no other" (157). Such religious conversion might not have been a primary goal of de Vaca's original expedition (gold, not God, was the central topic of his initial conversations with natives), and it certainly is not on the agenda of these slave traders, but it remains, particularly when coupled to obedience to Charles, a distinctly European cultural goal. But if de Vaca foregrounds that cultural goal and perspective in his narrative's introduction of this reconnection to Christians, his experiences throughout the encounter with them reveal that his identity and culture have been transformed into something quite distinct from theirs.

Those distinctions are immediately evident upon his first specific encounter with any of the group; these "four Christians on horseback . . . experience great shock upon seeing [de Vaca] so strangely dressed and in the company of Indians," and "remain looking at [him] a long time, so astonished that they neither [speak] to [him] nor manage to ask [him] anything" (159–60). This moment interestingly mirrors de Vaca's first postshipwreck encounter with natives, where his strange appearance and inability to speak their language caused similarly strong emotional responses. Of course, de Vaca does speak the same language as these Christians (although he has learned at least six other native languages during his time in the New World), and so once the moment passes he is able to tell them to take him to their captain, Diego de Alcaraz. But when de Vaca appears before Alcaraz and, more precisely, when the whole of his new cross-cultural community encounters Alcaraz and his men, the resulting encounter is even more fraught with identity and cultural confusion, and it is worth quoting at length. De Vaca has asked his tribe to bring food to the encounter, and when they arrive he finds that

> they brought us everything else they had, but we refused to take any of it except the food. And we gave everything else to the Christians so that they could distribute it among themselves. And after this we suffered many annoyances and great disputes with them, because they wanted to enslave the Indians we brought with us. And with this anger, on parting we left many Turkish bows that we carried, and many leather pouches and arrows and among them the five made from emeralds that we inadvertently left, and thus we lost them. . . . We had great difficulty convincing the Indians to return to their homes and secure themselves and sow their maize. They did not want but to go with us until leaving us with other Indians, as they were accustomed to doing, because if they returned without doing this, they feared they would die, and going with us, they feared neither the Christians nor their lances. The Christians were disturbed by this, and they made their interpreter tell them that we were of the same people as they, and that we had been lost for a long time, and that we were people of ill fortune and no worth, and that they were the lords of the land whom the Indians were to serve and obey. But of all this the Indians were only superficially or not at all convinced of what they told them. Rather, some talked with others among themselves, saying that the Christians were lying, because we came from where the sun rose, and they from where it set; and that we cured the sick, and that they killed those who were well; and that we came naked and barefoot, and they went about dressed and on horses and with lances; and that we did not covet anything but rather, everything they gave us we later returned and remained with nothing, and that the others had no other objective but to steal everything they found and did not give anything to anyone. And in this manner, they conveyed everything about us and held it in high esteem to the detriment of the others. (161–62)

There are numerous complexities within this climactic passage—and it is in many ways the climax of de Vaca's narrative, or at least of his experiences with the natives—but I would highlight three particularly significant details. First, it is important to remember that de Vaca began his captivity having "lost everything" he "carried" and become simply the possession of others; here he again loses possessions, but this time they represent the native cultures (despite the name, Turkish bows were weapons common to Southwestern tribes) and are lost to Europeans who seek (as the "lords of the land") to possess the natives and, implicitly but quite possibly, de Vaca as well. Second, it is worth noting that the Christians recognize and attempt (if for entirely selfish reasons) to define de Vaca and his men's hybrid identity, to explain how they are on the one hand "of the same people" but on the other distinct (and, in this formulation, lesser) in their identity because of their many years "lost" in the New World. Third, and most significant by far, is the extended native response to that definition, one that de Vaca privileges textually by including it at more than twice the length of the Christians' statements. Like the Christians, the natives differentiate de Vaca and his men from the other Europeans without arguing for a fully native identity either; instead, they too identify the men principally through their New World experiences, both literal (their appearances, their treatment of the natives) and spiritual (their role within the native mythology and beliefs). Along with the obvious difference in tone, it is crucial to note that de Vaca describes the natives here as "convey[ing] everything about us"—a tacit but quite striking agreement with the native perspective, perhaps the clearest indication anywhere in this passage that it is the native community to which his hybrid identity is most fully linked (not only by the two opposing parties but in his own perspective and narrative) throughout the encounter.

Given that encounter's complexity and confusion, what follows over the narrative's remaining pages can, on one level, be described as a retreat into a more fixed, simple cultural identity. Despite their confrontational early relationship to Alvaraz and his group, de Vaca and his men nonetheless accompany them for the remainder of their time in the New World; while they continue to encounter and interact with native tribes, their cross-cultural community has been disbanded, and the encounters feel much more like those from the narrative's opening section, where the expedition's explorers were sizing up the natives as potential subjects or conquests. And de Vaca makes in this section his first explicit address to Charles V since very early in the narrative, and does so in direct relationship to those questions of conquest: he prays that "God our Lord in his infinite mercy grant, in all the days of Your Majesty and under your authority and domination, that these people come and be truly and with complete devotion subject to the true Lord who created and redeemed them" (168). Despite the gentler goal here than Alvaraz's slave trading, "authority and domination" makes clear that there would be no role in this future New World for the many native "lords" and healers who had so influenced de Vaca's decade of experiences.

Nor, it seems, is there a role in that New World for de Vaca himself; he soon sets sail for Spain again, finds himself part of various nautical encounters with French and Portuguese vessels and thus quite explicitly a Spanish naval officer once more, and closes his own narrative (followed by an appendix in which he provides additional information on what happened to other expedition members) with his arrival back in Europe, ten years after the Narváez expedition's departure.

Yet de Vaca does not entirely abandon his ethnographic narrative role in these final pages, and it is in the text's concluding, most cross-cultural ethnographic moment that we can perceive some of the ways in which the hybrid identities contained in de Vaca's traveling tribe will continue to influence all the individuals and cultures experiencing life in the New World. De Vaca and his men have been speaking to a number of natives—who had fled from Alcaraz but return to speak with de Vaca, another indication of his closer ties to the native communities—about their Christian beliefs, and then ask the natives to articulate their own belief system more explicitly. And the resulting conversation, one of the last times in the narrative when de Vaca includes native voices, indicates at least the potential for continued cross-cultural conversations and transformations:

> To this they responded to the interpreter that they would be very good Christians and serve God. And when asked to what they gave reverence and made sacrifices and whom they asked for water for their maize fields and health for themselves, they responded that it was to a man who was in the sky. We asked them what his name was. And they said it was *Aguar,* and that they believed that he had created the whole world and all the things in it. We again asked them how they knew this. And they responded that their fathers and grandfathers had told it to them, that for a long time they had known about this, and they knew that that man sent water and all good things. We told them that the one to whom they referred we called God, and that thus they should call him and serve and adore him as we commanded and they would be well served by it. They responded that they understood everything very well and that thus they would do it. (166)

This is not, of course, an objective ethnographic interview by any standards; de Vaca and his men have a clear and culturally based religious goal and, as the word "commanded" implies, are happy to push the natives toward that goal. But neither is this Columbus renaming the islands in Spanish, with only a faint, immediately elided understanding that they are already known to the natives by other names. The interviewers here are willing and able to understand not only the linguistic but also the generational and cultural natures of the natives' voices and beliefs, and seem genuinely interested in finding a way for them to connect those aspects of their identities to parallel ones in their own experiences and cultures. If this remains a form of European exploration, it is certainly a much more sympathetic and cross-cultural one than those comprised by Alcaraz's slave-trading mission, Columbus's first voyage, or the initial Narváez expedition.

Since those latter kinds of exploration were far more typical than de Vaca's admittedly extreme decade of New World experience, it would be fair to ask whether cross-cultural conversations and transformations were possible, much less actual, for most of this era and its various cultures. But as Columbus's two letters indicate, the goals of European exploration and the realities of its effects—on the New World, on its native cultures, and even on the explorers' own identities and cultures—were always to a significant degree distinct. Certainly many of those effects were, as was the case for much of de Vaca's decade of experience, negative, threatening, and too often ultimately destructive to one or more of the cultures involved. Yet exploration's effects were also, at their core, deeply transformative—none of the individuals who experienced them, nor any of the cultures from which those individuals originated, would end the exploration process with the same identities with which they had begun it. And what de Vaca's experiences reveal, not because of their extreme nature but rather because they provide an extended and particularly explicit case study of processes that were taking place throughout the exploration era, is how fully cross-cultural those transformations were, and how much the evolving conversations between and shifts across distinct cultural identities influenced the formation of new, hybrid American identities in the centuries to follow.

2

Unsettling Transformations

Mary Rowlandson's Removes

Much of the early material in William Bradford's *Of Plymouth Plantation*, and particularly the crucial chapters between chapter 9 (the Mayflower's 1620 sighting of and landing at Cape Cod) and chapter 28 (the Pequot War of 1637), defines the New World's land and identity, and those people already inhabiting it, as explicitly alternative and opposed to both that which the Pilgrims have left behind and their own community and mission. These definitions are most famously found in the initial description of the New World in chapter 9:

> Being thus passed the vast ocean, and a sea of troubles before in their preparation . . . they had now no friends to welcome them nor inns to entertain or refresh their weatherbeaten bodies; no houses or much less towns to repair to, to seek for succor. It is recorded in Scripture as a mercy to the Apostle and his shipwrecked company, that the barbarians showed them no small kindness in refreshing them, but these savage barbarians, when they met with them . . . were readier to fill their sides full of arrows than otherwise. And for the season it was winter, they that know the winters of that country know them to be sharp and violent, and subject to cruel and fierce storms, dangerous to travel to known places, much more to search an unknown coast. Besides, what could they see but a hideous and desolate wilderness, full of wild beasts and wild men—and what multitudes there might be of them they knew not. (60–61)

Certainly the contrasts in the land itself, the absence of all civilized comforts and presence of only the harshest and most threatening wilderness, contribute to the entirely hostile first impression of America. But I would argue that the most striking contrast is that with Scripture—the Pilgrims have it so rough that they even outstrip their holy models—and here it is the uniquely savage nature of the New World's native inhabitants that provides the opposition. Moreover, while the land's hostilities are substantially linked to the season, and so at least somewhat transient in nature, the numberless multitudes of wild men pose a much more permanent threat to the Pilgrims' community and goals. And it is precisely the native cultures who will represent in Bradford's history the most significant and ongoing contrast and threat to the Pilgrim mission over its first few decades: from the next chapter's violent "First Encounter" (as the Pilgrims name the battle's site, thus setting the tone for all subsequent encounters as well) where "it please[s] God to vanquish their enemies and give them deliverance" (64); to the account in chapter 28 of the Pequot War, which begins "In the fore part of this year, the Pequots fell openly upon the English at Connecticut, in the lower parts of the river, and slew sundry of them as they were at work in the fields, both men and women, to the great terror of the rest, and went away in great pride and triumph, with many high threats," and maintains that tone throughout the chapter (80). The Pilgrims may indeed have perceived themselves as being on an errand into the wilderness, but the wild men at the heart of that land are often constructed by Bradford as a culture against, not among, and certainly not for which the English must struggle.

Yet Bradford's chronicle is likewise aware of and sensitive to the wide variety of other obstacles confronting the English settlers, and so this opening section also engages, in occasional but significant moments, with the concurrent role that native individuals and cultures played in helping the community survive its early, darkest period in the New World. Chapter 11, which begins the text's second book and opens with the community's most symbolic event, the signing of the Mayflower Compact, also introduces the most prominent such native presence, Squanto. The passage's opening sentence makes clear that accepting native assistance would not be easy for the Pilgrims, as it describes "the Indians" as "skulking about them," and once stealing "away their tools where they had been at work." But the next sentence explicitly transitions away from that perspective, beginning with a "but" and narrating the arrival of Samoset, who speaks to the Pilgrims "in broken English, which they [can] well understand but marvel at it." That cross-cultural starting point foreshadows the multiple ways in which Samoset will be "profitable" to the Pilgrims not only through his knowledge of the region but also and especially through introducing them to Squanto, "a native of this place, who had been in England and [can] speak better English than" Samoset. Squanto's most vital contributions to the Pilgrim community are practical ones—he "direct[s] them how to set their corn, where to take fish, and to procure other commodities, and [is] also their pilot to bring them to unknown places for their profit"—which Bradford describes from a culturally driven perspective, calling Squanto "a special instrument sent of God for their good beyond their expectation." Yet a native fulfilling that spiritual role is already a distinct shift from the other early encounters, and Squanto likewise alters the community's relationship to the native cultures more broadly: he introduces them to a local Wampanaog chief, Massasoit, with whom the Pilgrims make a six-point "peace" that Bradford notes has "now continued this 24 years" (68–69). From the foundational moments of English settlement in New England, then, there was a native presence not just outside, but among, the Pilgrim community, and neither that community, the native cultures, nor the cross-cultural interactions between the two could remain uninfluenced by that presence. In fact, as Cynthia Van Zandt has recently and powerfully demonstrated, "the [early settlement] period is remarkable for the scope and degree of cultural and political experimentation people attempted" (6–7).[1]

As the seventeenth century passed and the English communities in New England became more settled and stable, it would follow that the dependent, cross-cultural relationships with native cultures would be less necessary and thus less visible than the more explicitly opposed and hostile ones. Certainly the events of a half-century after the initial landing, the bloody and climactic 1675 to 1676 conflict between the English and the Wampanoags, which came to be known as King Philip's War, reflect those hostile relationships.[2] Similarly, the personal narrative of Mary Rowlandson, an English settler taken captive after the February 1675/76[3] attack on her village of Lancaster and held by the Wampanoags for 11 weeks, highlights in many ways the cultural chasm between the native and English communities and identities; that gap is largely based, just as it is in so much of Bradford's writing, on Rowlandson's devout Christian faith and worldview (as she articulates it both during her captivity and in her narration of it, composed and published six years later), but it is certainly exacerbated by the often brutal treatment that she and her fellow captives receive from their captors. These two communities are at war, after all, and so Rowlandson's identity, as a captive of a foreign and hostile culture, remains much more fixed than Cabeza de Vaca's (and moreover has a far shorter period in which to evolve). Yet that identity nonetheless includes two distinct characteristics that contribute to tentative and partial but still meaningful cross-cultural transformations in Rowlandson's perspective: her dependence on the natives for survival, which leads her to participate in their customs and practices more than she would otherwise have chosen to; and, much more complex and transformative, her use of particular skills (such as sewing) to become a viable part of the tribe's economic and social structures and identity.

As was the case with de Vaca's New World journey, Rowlandson's captivity experiences can thus exemplify the necessary and intricate cultural relationships that underlay and defined the settlement era. As Christopher Castiglia has argued, the narratives produced by such captives "persistently explore generic and cultural changes, divisions, and differences occasioned by the captives' cultural crossings" (4–5).[4] In some ways, Rowlandson's narrative reflections on her experiences allowed her to crystallize core elements of her Puritan beliefs and identity, and in the process, as Nancy Armstrong and Leonard Tennenhouse (1992) argue, help originate the modern English literary tradition.[5] But just as the foundational native presence in the English communities changed both cultures' identities, notwithstanding the wars that would all too soon divide and devastate those cultures, so too are both Rowlandson and her captors (including even King Philip himself) permanently influenced by their cross-cultural experiences; influences that her narrative, despite its overtly English and Christian perspective, depicts in subtle but significant moments and ways.

The title and peripheral materials of the narrative's first (1682) edition, along with the text's opening section, in no way foreshadow those transformations, highlighting instead on multiple levels the narrative's fixed Puritan cultural framework. The main title of that original edition, *The Sovereignty and Goodness of God*, in fact foregrounds Rowlandson's Christian themes to the exclusion of even their specific historical (much less cultural) contexts. The edition's title page does provide those contexts, however, and does so in such a way as to construct both the text's content and its goals in direct connection to that particular, culturally driven spiritual perspective. The work's subtitle, *The Narrative of the Captivity and Restoration of Mrs. Mary Rowlandson*, drives home the fortunately transient nature of Rowlandson's identity as a captive, while the subsequent paragraph of further explanation focuses on how Rowlandson was "treated in the most barbarous and cruel Manner by those vile Savages." If the cultural distinction and hostility are not clear enough, above that paragraph and in the center of the page is an illustration of a woman (presumably Rowlandson) with a rifle in hand, defending her home from four leering, distinctly devilish natives and their raised hatchets and rifles. No reader encountering this page would be left with any doubt as to the relationship between Rowlandson's identity and community and the native culture threatening both. And for those readers, the page's final paragraph makes clear the narrative's communal religious purpose, highlighting how, despite Rowlandson's intention that her text be "for her private Use," she has been convinced by "the earnest Desire of some Friends" to publish the narrative "for the Benefit of the afflicted." These opening identifiers, then, position both Rowlandson's experiences and her text as originating from and meant for a Puritan, or at least a Christian, cultural perspective.

Rowlandson's choices and emphases throughout the narrative's opening section drive home that shared, unified cultural framework. One of her most significant such choices is the very first one: to begin the narrative without a single word of introduction (of herself, the historical or geographic setting of her narrative, or any broader context), but rather with an opening sentence devoted entirely to the specifics of the attack on Lancaster. That sentence, "On the 10th of February, 1675, came the Indians with great numbers upon Lancaster: their first coming was about sun-rising; hearing the noise of some guns, we looked out; several houses were burning, and the smoke ascending to heaven," certainly hooks the reader and creates an immediate level of tension that will be sustained throughout the text (3). Yet I would argue that those effects are incidental, and that Rowlandson's choice is instead an instinctive and cultural one, guided not by the concerns of a prose stylist but by the shared communal knowledge she assumes between herself and her audience. And unlike de Vaca, who explicitly directed his narrative to an individual (his king) with whom that shared knowledge was obvious, Rowlandson's choice is apparently driven not by her text's publishing situation—the first authorized edition of the narrative was published in post-Restoration London, a community where Puritans constituted a distinct minority and those familiar with Massachusetts and its wars smaller still—but by her own identification with that particular, intimate audience.

As Rowlandson's opening section demonstrates, that shared cultural perspective unquestionably influences how she constructs both her narrative's principal content, her interactions with the Native Americans, and its overarching spiritual context. The section's images of the native attackers not only utilize the expected stereotypical phrases ("bloody heathens," "infidels," "murderous wretches") but also strip them of both humanity and agency. Rowlandson's diction throughout the passage depicts the natives as wild animals more than human adversaries: they are waiting outside a house to "devour" the Puritans; they are like "ravenous bears"; they leave the "Christians lying in their blood, . . . like a company of sheep torn by wolves." The latter phrase's simile actually disappears in the section's climactic paragraph, which turns the natives into the inhuman beasts to which they have been compared: Rowlandson describes the town's dead Puritans as "stripped naked by a company of hell-hounds . . . as if they would have torn our very hearts out." As illustrated by that sentence's main clause, Rowlandson consistently uses the passive tense throughout the section, focusing very fully on what is happening to her Puritan neighbors and minimizing the agency of these inhuman attackers in the process; the section's first paragraph, for example, contains five consecutive lengthy sentences with Puritan subjects, including the "five persons taken in one house," the "two others [who] were set upon," and so on. Even the day's horrific violence and total destruction, while certainly tied to the ferocity of these beastly creatures, is, Rowlandson makes clear, not due to their will. "Come, behold the works of the Lord, what desolations he has made in the earth," she writes, and the line creates a transition not only between the narrative of the attack and the description of its aftermath but also between the specific events and their broader, more explicitly communal spiritual context (3–9).

That spiritual frame, it is worth noting, is neither the only possible nor the most obvious communal context for this violence. The attack on Lancaster was one particularly brutal battle within a larger war, and that war likewise one conflict of all too many between the English settlers and the Native Americans. While Rowlandson chooses not to frame the narrative with any of that larger historical context, she does implicitly acknowledge it in the midst of her narration, writing, "Now is the dreadful hour come, that I have often heard of (in time of war, as was the case with others) but now mine eyes see it." Yet despite that heightened sense of the shared experience of war, the larger community to which Rowlandson consistently connects the day's specific events is defined instead by a shared Christian worldview. Describing for example the inability of the family's "six stout dogs" to repel the attacking natives, Rowlandson notes that "the Lord hereby would make us the more to acknowledge his hand, and to see that our help is always in him"; while the "us" being invoked here is on one level the family and village under attack, the sentence's shift to a perpetual present tense makes clear how much this perspective remains consistently accurate for a broader Christian community (5). Similarly, when Rowlandson introduces in the first section's closing pages her goals in writing the subsequent detailed captivity narrative, she does so through a telling scriptural parallel: she hopes to "better declare what happened to [her] during that grievous captivity," not in order to contribute to the history of King Philip's War or to a fuller understanding of Wampanoag culture (to cite two possible reasons), but because, like Job, she "only [is] escaped to tell the news" (8–9). Like that most put-upon Old Testament figure, Rowlandson will, she foreshadows here, be made by her God to suffer these difficulties, a typological link that separates her narrative very distinctly from its more specific historical contexts and causes. That is, while it will be the "barbarous creatures" who will literally lead her "up and down the wilderness," it is, Rowlandson argues, the Lord who "carrie[s her] along that [she] might see more of his power," an epiphany that, like Job's, would be impossible "had [she] not experienced it" (9, 12).

Much of Rowlandson's perspective in the narrative's first few "removes"[6]—both the past perspective she is attempting to recreate and the rhetorical one she takes in her writing—can be described as an attempt to find and reconnect with precisely such a Christian community. That search is entirely understandable, even inevitable, for someone in a condition like Rowlandson's; she sums up that condition at the end of the second remove: "My own wound also growing so stiff that I could scarce sit down or rise up; yet so it must be that I must sit all this cold winter night upon the cold snowy ground, with my sick child in my arms, looking that every hour would be the last of its life, and having no Christian friend near me, either to comfort or help me" (13). As her condition worsens over the next few removes, she responds by focusing more and more fully on making connections to her fellow Puritans, on at least three key levels. On her first night in the wilderness, she notices a "vacant house" nearby, one recently "deserted by the English," and asks her captors "whether I might lodge in the house that night" (10). When her mood is at its lowest point, she takes comfort in a brief encounter with a fellow captive, Robert Pepper, who has "been a considerable time with the Indians" and can empathize with her experiences (14). And when her young child succumbs to its injuries and dies, she resists the urge to "use wicked and violent means to end my own miserable life" by attempting to reconnect to her family, going to the "wigwam not very far off" where her daughter Mary is held captive (16–17).

Yet in each case Rowlandson's quest for community proves futile, and she places the blame for those failures squarely on the presence and perspective of the opposing, native community. Her captors deny her request to lodge in the English house, asking mockingly if she "will . . . love Englishmen still"; and instead of that potentially comfortable setting Rowlandson experiences "the dolefulest night that ever my eyes saw," as the natives make "the place a lively resemblance of hell" with their "roaring and singing and dancing and yelling" (10). When Rowlandson parts with Pepper, she sits "much alone," her only visitors the natives who "would come and tell me one hour, that my master will knock my child in the head, and then a second, and then a third" (15). Even when she comes "in sight" of her daughter Mary, the natives "would not let me come near," leaving Rowlandson with a new misery, that of a parent "ruled over" by "a nation which I knew not" (17). Exemplifying these opposed cultural perspectives is Rowlandson's brief relationship with the only other adult captive in her small group, Goodwife Joslin. At the end of the third remove, Rowlandson becomes a minister of sorts to Joslin, "ask[ing] her whether she would read" the Bible, and praying together over the verse of Psalm 27 that reads "Wait on the Lord, be of good courage, and he shall strengthen thine heart; wait I say on the Lord." Yet her ministry is ineffective: Joslin, who is late in pregnancy, cannot wait, "often asking the Indians to let her go home"; far from granting her request, the natives, "vexed with her importunity," perform what seems to be a ritual murder, singing and dancing about her naked body "in their hellish manner" and then throwing her and her young child into a fire to warn their fellow captives of the consequences "if they attempt to go home" (20–21).

Notwithstanding the inability of her religious fellowship with Joslin to save the woman from such a horrific fate, Rowlandson creates throughout her narrative a metatextual Christian community through her frequent allusions to and quotations from scripture. It is precisely in the third remove, with her child dead, her family increasingly distant, and these other Puritan relationships in danger, that Rowlandson includes the first five scriptural quotations in her captivity narrative; she included two quotations in her introductory section but none in the first or second removes. Fourteen of the remaining 17 removes will likewise feature at least one (and often multiple) quotations, elevating scripture to the level of a consistent intertext with Rowlandson's own voice and personal narrative. The literary concept of an intertext nicely captures the nature of Rowlandson's inclusion of these quotations: while it is certainly possible that a seventeenth-century Puritan woman would have the mindset and ability to make such scriptural allusions in the moment, it is also indisputably the case that the quotes themselves are provided by Rowlandson the author, reflecting on those moments and framing them through this rhetorical strategy. And that strategy helps create a Christian community on two levels: it extends and strengthens the effect of the introduction's Job parallel, drawing Rowlandson out of her specific individual experiences and linking her instead to the lives and perspectives represented by the Biblical figures; and it engages with a similarly broad potential audience, one defined not necessarily by any geographic or historical contemporaneity, but rather by its own scriptural knowledge and thus its ability to understand and appropriately contextualize the quotations.

The first scripture quotation in the captivity narrative seems to define this Christian community in explicit opposition to the native one in which she is being held. Rowlandson and her captors have arrived at "an Indian town called Wenimesset," and she witnesses in horror "the number of pagans (our merciless enemies) that . . . [come] about me!" She responds to this unfamiliar and threatening community by immediately turning to scripture, noting that she "might say as David, . . . I had fainted, unless I had believed, etc [sic]"; the final "etc" makes clear her reliance upon a Christian audience's ability to contextualize the quote beyond what she includes on the page. Moreover, her religious reflections do not end there, and she goes on to connect her past failures to honor the Sabbath to her present, decidedly non-Christian community; the memories of the former make it "easy for me to see how righteous it was with God to cut off the thread of my life, and cast me out of his presence forever" (13–14). So long as she is a part of communities such as Wenimesset, the moment's logic implies, she will be able only to imagine—and then to recreate through her narrative strategies— God's presence and the larger Christian community to which it can link her.

Yet one reason why Rowlandson can engage while in those communities with scriptural quotations at all—and the only reason she can read from scripture with Joslin—is the copy of the Bible in possession of which she subsequently finds herself in the third remove. And the way in which she comes to possess that Bible provides a compelling piece of evidence that Rowlandson's communities are neither as distinct nor as necessarily opposed as these early framings might indicate. Not only Rowlandson's narrative but the war itself has created that opposition, of course, and it is in fact another battle in that war that provides the initial frame for this moment, seemingly highlighting once again the cultural differences: the natives return from Medfield, "triumphing . . . over some Englishmen's scalps that they had taken (as their manner is) and brought with them." Yet scalps are not the only thing that the victors have brought back: "one of the Indians that came from [the] Medfield fight . . . brought some plunder," and he asks Rowlandson if she "would have a Bible," as he has "got one in his basket." Rowlandson does partly minimize the native's agency in performing this unexpected act of generosity, attributing it instead to "the wonderful mercy of God . . . in sending me a Bible." But she cannot entirely elide the question of the natives' own mercy, as illustrated by her asking the giver "whether he [thinks] the Indians would let me read it." The answer is a simple "yes," one proven immediately accurate as Rowlandson takes the Bible and consults a chosen passage (in Deuteronomy) on the spot (18–19).

Given the specific passage on which Rowlandson chooses to focus this first reading (Deuteronomy chapter 30, in which a "return to [the Lord] by repentance" is rewarded with further mercy in the form of "turn[ing] all those curses upon our enemies" [19]), as well as the similar and prominent role that such scriptural consultations play in the remainder of the narrative, it is tempting to read this moment as principally ironic (in ways that Rowlandson certainly does not acknowledge). Yet such a reading would depend on a static sense of Rowlandson's perspective on and in her two communities, a vision of her identity as consistently connected to the text's ideal but imagined Christian community, in direct opposition to the real but unrecognized native community represented by this gesture and gift. Similarly, that reading could note one symbolic resonance of Rowlandson's "removes," the ways in which she is being led further and further away from the Christian community. But there is another, more ambivalent—and potentially even positive—meaning of remove that would apply here: the removal, in Rowlandson's perspective, of the absolute cultural distinctions and hierarchies on which any vision of the natives as purely heathens or beasts would depend. And if she does not seem to recognize or follow through on that version of removal in this particular instance, the exchange does foreshadow the series of significant perspectival and cultural shifts that Rowlandson will undergo during, and as a direct result of, her captivity experience.

It is important to note that Rowlandson has cited minor but not insignificant examples of such shifts throughout the early portion of the narrative; in fact, at two of her very lowest points she does include (while understandably not dwelling at length on) examples of native actions that mitigate the depiction of their fundamental inhumanity. In the introduction, Rowlandson transitions directly from the brutal killings of her nephew and sister by "the infidels" to the much more civilized conversation that begins her captivity: "The Indians laid hold of us . . . and said, 'Come, go along with us.' I told them they would kill me. They answered, if I were willing to go along with them, they would not hurt me" (6–7). And in the third remove, when Rowlandson takes "the first opportunity I [can] get to go look after" the body of her dead child, she finds it missing; she asks the natives "what they [have] done with it" and they take her to the freshly dug grave where "they [have] buried it." Rowlandson follows this latter exchange by noting that "there I left that child in the wilderness, and must commit it, and myself also, in this wilderness condition to him who is above all" (16). Yet moments like these lessen the wildness of that wilderness, belying the beastliness of the unfamiliar but clearly civilized culture into the care of which Rowlandson is ever more fully committed throughout this section.

Rowlandson highlights her increasing immersion in that native culture in the brief (one-paragraph) sixth remove, noting that "if one looked before one there was nothing but Indians, and behind one, nothing but Indians, and so on either hand, I myself in the midst and no Christian soul near" her. Just as the final clause suggests that Rowlandson is still searching for a Christian community at this moment in her captivity, so too does a scriptural allusion earlier in the paragraph link her to yet another typological predecessor, this time a model of communal separation: "I went along that day mourning and lamenting, leaving farther my own country, and travelling into the vast and howling wilderness, and I understood something of Lot's wife's temptation, when she looked back" (25–26). Yet wherever Rowlandson looks, whether literally or spiritually, she cannot alter the reality of her surroundings, and in one small but telling way it is her perspective instead that begins to shift in this section of the narrative. After narrating in the fifth remove a time when she drinks "the broth" produced when the natives "boil an old horse's leg," Rowlandson steps back to acknowledge the broader shift in her culinary attitudes of which that moment is a part: "The first week of my being among them I hardly ate anything; the second week I found my stomach grow very faint for want of something, and yet it was very hard to get down their filthy trash. But the third week, though I could think how formerly my stomach would turn against this or that, and I could starve or die before I could eat such things, yet they were very sweet and savory to my taste" (23–24). There are a few significant formal choices within this short passage that contribute to the sense of shift here. One has to do with the sentence structure—the first and second weeks' perspectives are linked together, as two stages of a still decidedly English view on the natives' "filthy trash," by the semicolon; whereas the third week's perspective is distinguished from them through the creation of a new sentence, one that begins with "but" to make the transition explicit. Moreover, the second sentence's multiple time periods drive home the shift, with the English perspective in the narrative's past, one still remembered ("I could think how formerly") yet all the more past as a result. And in introducing the new perspective in the final clause, Rowlandson makes clear how much it is part of an individual shift based on her own experiences—the food might still be "filthy trash" from that communal, English vantage point, but it is nonetheless "sweet and savory to my taste."

Food similarly contributes to an even more complex moment of shift in the brief but dense seventh remove. Rowlandson frames the remove's events as "a grievous day of travel," and while part of that grief is due to her physical circumstances—"fatigue and soreness of body"—part is produced instead by a series of reminders of the community and perspective she has left behind: she sees "a place where English cattle had been: that [is] a comfort to me, such as it" is; they pass "an English path which so [takes] with me that I [think] I could have freely lain down and died"; and later they arrive at an area of "deserted English fields," the "forsaken and spoiled" state of which is "a solemn sight" for Rowlandson. Yet despite her continued attachment to these traces of an English presence, Rowlandson indicates here an encroaching native presence on two distinct but interconnected levels. In her own perspective, her culinary tastes continue to evolve: spotting a native carrying "a basket of horse-liver," Rowlandson surprises him by asking for a piece; he questions whether she "can . . . eat horse-liver," but she vows that she will try, and in fact she ends up eating it "half ready, . . . with the blood about my mouth, and yet a savory bit it [is] to me." Moreover, while to Rowlandson as an individual this remove thus marks another sign of the shrinking gap between an English and a native perspective, her language in describing food in this section points to the artificiality of that gap on a communal level. The crops that once occupied those forsaken and spoiled fields were "wheat and Indian corn," and the latter phrase in particular is repeated three times in the remove's one paragraph; Rowlandson herself gets "two ears of Indian corn," and is then "troubled" when "one of them [is] stolen from me." The phrase provides an explicit reminder of the ways in which the seeds provided by natives like Squanto had significantly contributed to both the English settlers' initial survival and their subsequent sustenance; and indeed Rowlandson's casual use of the phrase, and her sense of the crop as one that now belongs to the English fields (and one that it requires no shift in perspective for her to consume), only heightens how fully such native influences had been integrated into the English community in the half-century since those initial encounters (26–27).

It is, however, to the much more partial but still striking reverse process—Rowlandson's integration into the native community—that the narrative turns in the next two removes. The long and hugely significant eighth remove opens with a paragraph in which Rowlandson's search for a Christian community, both during her captivity and in the text, seems to meet with striking success. At a moment of pause in the journey, Rowlandson's "son Joseph unexpectedly [comes] to me"; while the two are compelled to acknowledge "the change that had come upon us," they nonetheless reconnect over a brief but powerful shared reading of scripture. And Rowlandson then steps back to write one of her most explicitly metatextual reflections on her rhetorical choices and strategies, noting that she will "take occasion to mention one principal ground of my setting forth these lines: . . . to declare the works of the Lord. . . . And his goodness in bringing to my hand so many comfortable and suitable scriptures in my distress" (28). If the meeting with Joseph has reminded Rowlandson of her separated but not lost Christian community, it also seems to provide her with a particularly strong impetus to consider how her text can further strengthen that community's perspective.

Yet Rowlandson transitions back to the captivity narrative itself, at the opening of the next paragraph, with the phrase "but to return," and her choice of words is particularly apt; in the remainder of the remove she will return to the native community very fully, and in fact much more meaningfully than in any prior moment. That reconnection begins with what appears to be another instance of cultural conflict: Rowlandson finds herself "sitting alone in the midst" of a "numerous crew of pagans," and their "rejoic[ing] over their gains and victories" is a tipping point for her emotional state; her "heart [begins] to fail and I [fall] a-weeping, . . . the first time to my remembrance that I wept before them." Since Rowlandson acknowledges that up until this moment she "could not shed one tear in their sight," it is possible that her breakdown humanizes her for the natives, makes her something more than a captured enemy. And likewise the native response to her tears humanizes them for her, through both words and deeds: first, one asks her why she is crying, and when she answers that "they would kill me," he replies "No, none will hurt you." And his comrades' actions give proof to the claim, with one giving Rowlandson "two spoonfuls of meal to comfort" her, and another giving her "half a pint of peas, which [is] worth more than many bushels at another time" (29). Rowlandson's choices in both the latter phrases represent significant shifts in her perspective in response to these kindnesses: her recognition that the gifts are to comfort her, and thus her ability to see the natives as sympathetic to her situation; and her acknowledgment of the worth of those gifts, and thus her understanding that the members of this community have the power not only to threaten or treat her as a captive foe but also to make her feel more like a foreign but welcome, and even valued, guest.

Building on that latter role but taking it to an even more unexpected and socially significant level is the remove's subsequent event, one introduced in the striking next sentence: "Then I went to see King Philip." Rowlandson has already mentioned that her master (on whom more below) is a relative of the Wampanoag chief, but nonetheless this surprising encounter with the war's namesake has three immediate effects: implicitly, it foregrounds the broader historical contexts of Rowlandson's individual experiences; but explicitly and more importantly, it both humanizes this most overt native enemy and makes clear that Rowlandson is, to the Wampanoags, more than just a prisoner of war. Those latter two effects are immediately apparent, as Philip bids Rowlandson "come in and sit down, and ask me whether I would smoke [a pipe]." Rowlandson does not explicitly acknowledge the tremendous social value attached by the Wampanoag tribe to smoking (in any circumstance, much less with the chief), but she does admit that the gesture represents "a usual compliment now-a-days amongst saints and sinners"; the request certainly indicates Philip's sense of Rowlandson as at least a valued guest and, potentially, a member of the community. Her response, not coincidentally, is based not at all on cultural differences or perspectives, and instead simply on the personal fact that she has given up smoking and has no wish to resume the "bewitching" habit. And the communal connection that both Philip's offer and her personal response intimate is directly borne out in the next paragraph— Rowlandson opens it by noting the preparations for the next stage in war between the natives and her English compatriots, as "the Indians gather their forces to go against Northampton," but makes no further comment about that conflict, focusing instead on the continued shifts in her social role on the native home front (29–30).

That expanding role begins with additional and even more socially significant gestures from Philip. He asks Rowlandson "to make a shirt for his boy, which I did, for which he gave me a shilling." Perhaps unable to recognize immediately the potential shift in status from captive to servant implied by this act, Rowlandson "offer[s] the money to my master"—but he provides further proof of that shifting role, as he bids her "keep it, and with it I bought a piece of horse flesh." This initial exchange is followed by another, extended one: Philip asks her "to make a cap for his boy, for which he invite[s] me to dinner"; and there he gives her "a pancake, about as big as two fingers." Despite the meal's size and its native preparation—"beaten and fried in bear's grease"—Rowlandson admits that she thinks she has "never tasted pleasanter meat in my life." Now her culinary changes in perspective are a part of a larger social fabric, one in which the wages she receives for her contributions to the community provide her with the opportunity to purchase her sustenance (rather than simply relying on charity). This sets off a series of such trades with multiple natives: a squaw asks her "to make a shirt for her sannup, for which she [gives Rowlandson] a piece of bear"; another asks her "to knit a pair of stockings for which she [gives Rowlandson] a quart of peas." While in some ways the absence of wages from these later exchanges could be read as confirming Rowlandson's outsider status in the community, it is also possible to read these moments as more intimate and communal still for that absence: the natives seem explicitly concerned with Rowlandson's hunger, and are allowing her to contribute her unique skills to the community in exchange for helping to relieve that condition. And in fact Rowlandson takes these gifts of food and makes them a part of another, extremely meaningful social gesture of her own: she "boil[s] my peas and bear together, and invite[s] my master and mistress to dinner" (30).

The mutual acts of kindness comprised by those exchanges represent, I would argue, the most central element of a community in which different perspectives can coexist in a genuine—rather than either a hostile or a forced—relationship. Such acts continue, on a number of different levels, through the remainder of the eighth and all of the ninth remove. Rowlandson is given "one spoonful of meal," and although at first it seems that "somebody [steals] it" from her pocket, that anonymous philanthropist in fact "put[s] five Indian corns in the room of it, which [are] the greatest provisions I had in my travel for one day" (31). Learning that her son is "now about a mile from" her, Rowlandson "ask[s] liberty to go and see him," and is granted that opportunity; when she gets lost along the way, all the natives she encounters aid her on her journey, with "not one . . . offer[ing] the least imaginable miscarriage" (33). Such thorough kindness has a tangible effect on Rowlandson's perspective, as she lets her guard down and views the native community as full of potential sources of support: finding herself still in need of "something to satisfy my hunger," Rowlandson wanders "among the wigwams"; and despite the fact that all the natives she meets are "strangers to me that I never saw before," they extend the streak of communal response, offering not only food but even to "buy me if they [are] able." And the shift in perspective engendered by these welcoming attitudes is, Rowlandson's narrative makes clear, a permanent one: "I cannot but think how pleasant it was to me," she writes after one such exchange, and while "cannot but think" indicates her hesitancy to acknowledge the pleasantness of these communal connections, the sentence's present tense nonetheless extends that acknowledgment into her memories of this period (34).

While a number of natives—from King Philip himself to these anonymous but equally welcoming strangers—have helped create these positive shifts and memories, Rowlandson makes clear that her strongest communal connection is that which she develops with her master. He is, Rowlandson argues, "the best friend that I had of an Indian, both in cold and hunger" (37). Part of that connection is without question due to her master's sympathetic awareness of Rowlandson's pain at being separated from her family, and especially her husband; she asks at the opening of the twelfth remove "whether he would sell me to my husband," and he answers her "*Nux* [yes], which [does] much rejoice my spirit" (36). Yet there is also something comforting about the man's simple presence, a lessening of the most negative aspects of her condition—such as the aforementioned cold and hunger—when she is with him. When he leaves for a time with his wife, Rowlandson finds herself unable to reach that state of comfort: "Down I sat with my heart as full as it could hold and yet so hungry that I could not sit neither" (37). After attempting to alleviate that hunger, Rowlandson is once again reminded that her "master himself was gone and me left behind so that my spirit was now quite ready to sink"; even her most dependable remedy cannot lighten her perspective, as she takes her "Bible to read, but . . . [finds] no comfort here neither, which many times I was wont to find" (40). In moments such as these, it is possible to imagine that if their respective marital situations and ages were different, Rowlandson and her master might have moved toward one of those cross-cultural romantic relationships, and subsequent tribal adoptions, that were the occasional result of English captivities; it is perhaps due to the depth of their connection that Rowlandson's mistress wants very little to do with her and treats her more harshly than any other member of the community. When Rowlandson cooks the two of them dinner in the eighth remove, for example, "the proud gossip . . . would eat nothing, except one bit that he gave her upon the point of his knife" (30–31); later her mistress finds her reading the Bible and "snatche[s] it hastily out of my hand and [throws] it out of doors" (36).

Rowlandson engages with both of these elements of her captivity—the possibility of a permanent future with the tribe on the one hand, and the limit on community and cultural understanding represented by her mistress on the other—in the long thirteenth remove. She admits that her desire to reconnect with the English community remains strong but also notes that it might never be fulfilled, narrating how "about this time I began to think that all my hopes of restoration would come to nothing" (40). Moreover, she makes clear in a very complex passage that those desires represent a part of her past, one for which there is not necessarily a place in her shifted situation and community: "And here I cannot but remember how many times sitting in their wigwams and musing on things past, I should suddenly leap up and run out as if I had been at home, forgetting where I was and what my condition was. But when I was without and saw nothing but wilderness and woods and a company of barbarous heathens, my mind quickly returned to me" (39–40). Certainly Rowlandson's word choices here exemplify the cultural oppositions that have been a part of her English perspective from the text's opening: "home" on the one hand, "wilderness" and "barbarous heathens" on the other. Just as certainly, her subsequent response to the death of her mistress's child highlights how genuine the gulf remains between her perspective and that of the native community: despite having lost her own child only weeks before, Rowlandson notes of this loss that "there was one benefit in it, that there was more room" in the wigwam. Whatever the relationship between Rowlandson and her mistress, her professed inability to "much console with" the group of mourners who gather to bury the papoose does her no credit (45). Yet I would argue that the kindnesses shown to Rowlandson throughout the prior several removes, and the resulting and significant shifts in her role within and perspective on the native community, provide explicit evidence that were she in fact to remain with the tribe for the rest of her life, such cultural gaps would continue to narrow. Moreover, if her master had been present at this moment of loss, or if it were Philip's son (for whom Rowlandson had made the shirt and cap) who died—if, that is, the loss were to a part of the particular, fledgling community to which Rowlandson has already developed connections—it seems likely that she would have reciprocated to those natives the sympathetic responses she had received from them.

Those communal connections continue to develop, in small and partial but telling ways, over the next few removes. In the fourteenth remove, Rowlandson sleeps away a rainy night in the comfort of a "dry bark wigwam" and awakens to see that "many of them had lain in the rain all night"; she does attribute this small blessing to the Lord's mercy, but also admits that "they were so nice in other things" (47). In the fifteenth remove her communal exchanges resume, with one of the natives giving her "a pipe, another a little tobacco, another a little salt, which I would change for a little victuals"; those victuals cannot entirely alleviate Rowlandson's "starving condition," but she does note that "sometimes it fell out that I got enough and did eat until I could get no more" (48). And two small details in the seventeenth remove illustrate how these small communal gestures and their accompanying perspective shifts have become an assumed part of Rowlandson's experiences with the tribe. Having stopped for the night in an "Indian town," Rowlandson enters a random wigwam to find a native "boiling of horse's feet," and when she asks for "a little of his broth or water," he offers "as much broth as" she wants; the shared meal is enough to make her "spirit [come] again." Moreover, Rowlandson also feels welcome to participate in the broader communal exchanges taking place in the town: "The Indians sat down by a wigwam, discoursing, but I was almost spent and could scarce speak" (50–51). While all of these details reflect continuing realities of Rowlandson's situation—exposure to the natural elements, hunger, fatigue—it is fair to say that those realities are not limited to Rowlandson, and in fact are shared across this wartime native community. Moreover, she is treated by the natives as and feels herself to be a member of that community, experiencing both those difficulties and the small comforts that can lessen them at the end of a long day's travels.

By this time, those travels are winding their way back toward the geographic starting point of Rowlandson's captivity, and thus toward the twentieth remove's redemption by her husband and return to the English community. But before her captivity and narrative reach that concluding section, she provides in the nineteenth remove a series of striking final pieces of evidence for the complex, ongoing shifts in her communal role and perspective. The remove opens with Rowlandson at a low point both physically and emotionally—the group is walking through "a great swamp" and she feels as though she almost "should have sunk down at last and never get out," and that she has "indeed my life but little spirit." But those spirits are revived by the two members of the native community who have been most influential in effecting Rowlandson's shifts. First, Philip takes Rowlandson "by the hand" and conveys two pieces of good news: she will soon rejoin her English community, since "two weeks more and I shall be Mistress again"; but she will even sooner reconnect with her most positive native community, as "quickly I shall come to my master again." Importantly, Rowlandson focuses here on the latter piece of news, transitioning directly to her arrival at "Wachusett where my [master is], and [how] glad I [am] to see him." And indeed her master immediately improves both her physical and emotional states: noting that she has not bathed this month, he "fetche[s] me some water himself," and then gives her both "a glass to see how I looked" and "something to eat." Rowlandson is "wonderfully revived with this favor showed me," reinforcing just how powerful her communal connections with Philip and, especially, her master have been in shifting the nature of her captivity experience (52–53).

Moreover, such encounters have also shifted her perspective on the native community overall, a shift reflected by Rowlandson's structural choices in this remove. She follows these positive exchanges with her narrative's longest and most objective ethnographic passage, on her master's relationships and living arrangements with his three squaws. The passage significantly complicates, on multiple levels, the negative vision of her mistress that Rowlandson has created in those earlier exchanges. For one thing, she provides a much fuller and more balanced portrayal of the woman: using her name, Weetamoo, for the first time; and highlighting the details of "her work ... mak[ing] girdles of wampum and beads." Moreover, framing Weetamoo in relationship to her husband's two other squaws makes clear the intricate gender relationships and power dynamics that constitute marriage in this particular community, while likewise introducing into the text another native benefactor: her master's oldest squaw, who "refreshe[s]" Rowlandson by offering her victuals whenever she wants them and making her a comfortable bed, "the first time I had any such kindness showed" her (53–54). This section of the remove thus creates a more fully humanized vision of the native community for both Rowlandson herself and for her audience, and makes clear that her master's kindness is a part of, rather than an exception to, the broader set of social relationships to which he belongs.

Rowlandson's next structural choice adds further levels of complexity and humanity to her portrayal of the native community. She transitions directly from this ethnographic paragraph into the arrival of "Tom and Peter," two "Christian Indians" who serve as go-betweens for the English and Wampanoag communities. This role links the men in some ways to Rowlandson herself, a parallel that she intimates by noting that "though they [are] Indians," she takes "them by the hand and burst[s] out into tears." Moreover, they provide an explicit link between her past and present communities—she "ask[s] them how my husband [does], and all my friends and acquaintances," and they provide her with her first update on those members of the English community. And her encounter with these men transitions directly into the narrative's most explicit portrayal of the Wampanoag political system, as Rowlandson is called to testify about the possibility of her redemption by the English before the "sagamores" who constitute the tribe's "General Court." That group rules, based entirely on her testimony, "that for twenty pounds I should be redeemed," and commissions "a praying-Indian" to write a letter to the English Council with those terms (54–56). Besides illustrating the parallel governing bodies and political frameworks present in these two warring communities, this section reiterates the earlier point that Rowlandson's voice and perspective have a presence within and the power to help direct the native community as well as her own relationship to it.

In the twentieth remove, as the English respond favorably to the Court's offer and their representative, John Hoar, arrives to negotiate (on behalf of both her husband and the Puritan Council) for Rowlandson's release, she returns not only in body but in perspective very fully to the Christian community. That is, even before the successful redemption and her reunion with her husband and extended family, Rowlandson structures this final remove around a return to the kinds of typological, religious contexts with which she had opened her captivity narrative. She dedicates eight long paragraphs in the middle of the remove, for example, to "mention[ing] a few remarkable passages of providence," five moments from throughout her captivity that symbolize from her Puritan perspective the Lord's hand in her life and experiences (66–70). And she concludes the remove with an extended, famous reflection on the spiritual meaning of her experiences, especially emphasizing God's agency in both creating her circumstances and manipulating their events in order to "scourge and chasten" her and "show me the vanity of . . . outward things" (79). Moreover, these spiritual conclusions are directly paralleled by Rowlandson and her family's full return to the English community on both specific and broad levels—despite having been left with no home or belongings by the Lancaster attack, the family creates a new home in Boston thanks to "the benevolence of Christian friends, some in this town, and some in that, and others, and some from England" (77). These various returns seem to reemphasize the cultural contrasts with which Rowlandson likewise opened her narrative and to which she returns in these closing pages, opposing her captivity "in the midst of thousands of enemies and nothing but death before" her to the "fatted calf" that represents her family's present state (78).

Yet Rowlandson remains in this concluding remove as honest a narrator as she has been throughout the text, and so she admits in one telling passage that those cultural contrasts do not quite conform to her individual experiences with and in the native community. "I have been in the midst of those roaring lions and savage bears that feared neither God nor man nor the devil," she begins that passage, seeming to return to the introduction's depictions of the natives' inhumanity. But in every version of that communal experience—"alone and in company, sleeping all sorts together"—she can attest that "not one of them ever offered me the least abuse of unchastity in word or action" (70–71). In fact what she was often offered, by many of them (from Philip to her master to men and women she would meet only once), was quite the opposite—communal sustenance and support. In the closing lines of the nineteenth remove, Rowlandson narrates a particularly illustrative moment of such support and its ability to undermine fixed cultural distinctions and hostilities. While she is sharing a meal with a native, another tells her that "he seems to be my good friend, but he killed two Englishmen at Sudbury and there lie their clothes behind" her. She looks and does indeed see the battle's remnants, "bloody clothes with bullet holes in them." But in her own experience, she continues, this same native "many times refreshed me: five or six times did he and his squaw refresh my feeble carcass. If I went to their wigwam at any time they would always give me something and yet they were strangers that I never saw before" (59–60). This native is no more absolutely defined by his military service against the English than King Philip is by the war that bears his name; both men are also members of a social community, one in which strangers can embrace and support a captive, making her, however transiently, into a meaningful part of that community as well.

Just over a year after Rowlandson's redemption, King Philip's War would end with the English triumphant, Philip himself dead, and the Wampanoags and their allies decimated. The war could be read as providing a decisive end not only to the six-point peace treaty signed by William Bradford's Pilgrims and Massasoit's Wampanoag tribe but also to the cross-cultural relationship of mutual respect and support represented by both that treaty and its native facilitator Squanto. The brutal attack with which Rowlandson's narrative opens, coupled with the cultural distinctions and prejudices that both her English perspective and the perspectives of her more cruel captors often include, can similarly exemplify both the historical events and the communal divisions that doomed such cross-cultural relationships to failure. Yet in the ways in which Rowlandson is removed from her English community and perspective and integrated, briefly but meaningfully, into the native ones, her narrative highlights as well the ongoing possibilities for genuine encounter and influence across these cultures. Just as the Pilgrims could not have survived and prospered in the New World without both the presence and the permanent influences of Squanto and his community, so too does Rowlandson owe her life and future to the support of natives like her master and Philip. Even more significantly, those moments when Rowlandson becomes a functioning and contributing member of the Wampanoag tribe reflect a distinct and unique potential New World community, one based on an unsettling of any absolute cultural perspectives in favor of connection and codependence. And by including those moments at length in her narrative, Rowlandson makes clear that she cannot but remember, and thus be influenced by, her removal to that alternative vision of culture and community.

3

Revolutionary Transformations

Olaudah Equiano's Fortunate Vicissitudes

Phillis Wheatley's "On Being Brought from Africa to America" (1773) emphasizes the concepts of cultural superiority and agency on which the incorporation of African American slaves into the Revolution's ideal images of American identity would seem to depend. Wheatley's opening four lines represent the title's two geographic and cultural entities as entirely opposed, principally through a chronological and spiritual hierarchy: Africa is the "pagan land" that birthed Wheatley's "benighted soul"; America the space that has induced her to know in the present and seek in the future "redemption" through her "God" and "Savior too." Moreover, that hierarchy is linked directly to Wheatley's passivity in the transition from one culture to the other, a passivity that in the ambiguous title could refer to the involuntary transit of the Middle Passage, but that the lines themselves reveal instead to be the hand of providence, the Lord's mercy bringing Wheatley to a superior culture and teaching her soul its spiritual perspective. And the subsequent four lines drive home and extend to a more communal level both of these initial elements: contrasting Wheatley's past racial identity, the culture of her "sable race" who are "black as Cain," with her present and future religious one, "th'angelic train" she hopes to "join"; and illustrating through the phrase "may be refined" that race's passive role in the redemption process (420–21). The hierarchical nature of culture may mean that all men are not created equal, the poem's speaker admits, but the interconnected, similarly ideal presences of America and Christianity can forcefully produce such equality.

The poem's seventh line does include one moment when the speaker takes on a more active role, through her direct command to her audience of "Christians" to "remember" that potential equalizing process (421). And Wheatley's identity and work as a poet overall, and more specifically the political uses to which she puts both her experiences and her voice in a number of her poems, highlight her ability to embrace actively a revolutionary American identity. In "To the Right Honorable William, Earl of Dartmouth" (1773), Wheatley makes an extended and powerful appeal to her British addressee on behalf of that revolutionary America. For most of the poem she does so through a speaker whose identity seems solely American, with no explicit racial or religious culture linked to that national identification; but in the metapoetic and hugely significant fourth stanza, she acknowledges that her "love of Freedom" and "wishes for the common good" have "sprung" directly from her experiences as a slave. Those experiences remain implicitly largely positive—her enslavement only "seeming cruel fate" and "Afric's happy seat" only "fancy'd"[1]—but they are here also foundational; that is, Africa and slavery no longer represent a dark past to be erased through enlightenment and refining, but compose instead elements of her individual identity ("such, such my case") that have contributed directly to her revolutionary American perspective (428–29). And in "To His Excellency, General Washington" (1775), Wheatley's speaker identifies even more fully and unapologetically with that American cultural identity, writing on direct behalf of all "Columbia" to implore this "great chief" to "proceed" with his revolutionary leadership. No longer merely a vessel for a superior Christian faith, America here constitutes its own distinct and ideal racial and religious culture, one Wheatley defines and celebrates as "the land of freedom's heaven-defended race" (427–28).

America's self-creation and self-definition in the Revolutionary era seemed at times to necessitate an elision of African slavery similar to that intimated in the first Wheatley poem's image of refinement. Before producing the final draft of the Declaration of Independence, for example, the Continental Congress deleted

Thomas Jefferson's entire paragraph addressing the issue of slavery, one that accused the King of "wag[ing] cruel war against human nature itself" and "violating its most sacred rights of life and liberty in the persons" of African slaves.[2]

But I would argue that there was throughout this foundational national moment a broader revolution taking place, one comprising the ability of Americans—individually and collectively—to embrace their own new identities, independent of the nations and cultures to which they had previously belonged. That revolutionary process of American identification is illustrated by Wheatley's latter two poems, but is exemplified at greater length and with significantly more complexity in the life and *Interesting Narrative* of Olaudah Equiano. Equiano creates in his narrative at least three distinct cultural identities: the very specific local identity of the kingdom of Benin into which he is born; a broader African identity that forms during his years of slavery and accompanies Equiano throughout the remainder of his life; and his most individualized and ideal identity, a transatlantic, globalized self present most explicitly in the mobile communities created during his many nautical voyages and adventures. Equiano consistently locates and defines that third identity in his ability to make and remake himself and his fortunes, and his concurrent refusal to settle too comfortably or absolutely into any static version of culture or self. And while this third identity includes without question some unsettling roles and perspectives, particularly in relation to Equiano's fellow Africans and slaves, it nonetheless represents a revolutionary, cross-cultural transformation in what the still-new world of America could include and mean in this founding moment.[3]

The veracity of the African birth and early life with which Equiano opens his narrative has, in recent years, been called into question. Scholar Vincent Carretta has unearthed documents (principally Equiano's English baptismal record and a Royal Navy muster roll) that suggest that Equiano was born in South Carolina, and thus that all the text's details about Africa and the Middle Passage (which compose the entirety of chapters 1 and 2) were fabricated, with the aid of sources such as other slaves' oral histories and texts by contemporary abolitionists like Anthony Benezet.[4] Certainly there are moments in those chapters, and particularly in the first chapter's description of Benin, that read more like a mythologized or imagined view of Africa than a firsthand account; for example, Equiano notes that his village had "plenty of Indian corn, and vast quantities of cotton and tobacco" (11), products associated at least as overtly with the American South as with the interior of Africa. Yet wherever Equiano was actually born—and scholars continue to debate the question—it is most relevant to my analysis that he chooses in his narrative to delineate the local and African identities on which these early chapters so fully focus. That is, Equiano's choice to ground his narrative and life in precisely these two cultures—the very stable and static origin point in Benin, and then the more fluid but still explicitly racial pan-African slave community—is profoundly foundational for his later portrayals of cross-cultural transformations and identities. As April Langley argues, in any case Equiano's "text can be said to be representative of an Afro-British American or African-descended identity searching for its African origins, real or imagined" (97).[5]

In the book's 1792 fifth (Edinburgh) edition, Equiano includes and responds to similar contemporary accusations about his birth (alleged to be "in the Danish island of Santa Cruz, in the West Indies") and the narrative's opening chapters. Those accusations had apparently arisen from proslavery quarters, and so both Equiano's own responses and those of the testimonials on his behalf tend to connect the veracity of his African origins directly to the book's most overt political purpose, its opposition to the slave trade. In that light, the testimonials in particular seek to define Equiano's present identity as still very much a version of the African one: Thomas Digges identifies Equiano as "an enlightened African"; William Langworth links that identity to his literary style, arguing that "the simplicity that runs through his Narrative is singularly beautiful, and that beauty is heightened by the idea that it is *true*"; and a favorable review of the book's first edition intertwines text and author even more fully in its assertion that "we entertain no doubt of the general authenticity of this very intelligent African's story. . . . The Narrative wears an honest face." Yet while Equiano does include among these peripheral materials a letter to Parliament in which he frames his text as "the production of an unlettered African," he elsewhere distances the elements of his past experiences from those of his present identity. For example, he ends the note "To the Reader" with which he prefaces the testimonials by appealing "to those numerous and respectable persons of character who knew me when I first arrived in England, and could speak no language but that of Africa." While he references that linguistic history in order to counter explicitly the "invidious falsehood" about his Caribbean heritage, it likewise implicitly illustrates how far the author of this note, and the entire narrative to follow, has come from that moment; how much, that is, his language and culture are now those of Africa and England and the journeys he has taken and self he has become, between and beyond both worlds. If, as he writes to Parliament, verifying his African origins can partly illustrate "the horrors of that trade [by which] I was first torn away from all the tender connections that were naturally dear to my heart," it can also—and more prominently in the narrative as a whole—illuminate why he "regard[s] myself as infinitely more than compensated by the introduction I have thence obtained" to that new world and identity (xxvii–xxxvii).

The first chapter of the narrative itself similarly modulates between Equiano's specific, originating national and racial cultures and the more individual identity toward which his life and text will move. The narrative opens with a metatextual paragraph in which Equiano reflects explicitly on the subject of "those who publish their own memoirs," and more exactly on the kind of identity and life that his memoir will depict. On the one hand, he is well aware that such a life will and to a degree must be viewed through the lens of his particular nation and race, and acknowledges that he likewise takes such a view: "Did I consider myself a European, I might say my sufferings were great; but, when I compare my lot with that of most of my countrymen, I regard myself as a *particular favorite of Heaven.*" Yet if Equiano does still compare his identity to those of his original rather than his adopted countrymen, the italicized phrase indicates that his self-conception is at the same time more individualized (not to mention more Christianized) than that. He in fact goes out of his way in this opening paragraph to frame himself not as a representative of any larger communal narrative, so much as "a private and obscure individual, and a stranger too." Moreover, as "stranger" might suggest, he is an individual whose personal narrative is distinguished from the more familiar experiences of the majority, however that broader community is defined: "There are a few events in my life which have not happened to many." And he ends the paragraph by stressing a textual goal much less specific than (for example) abolishing the slave trade, claiming that "the ends for which my [writing] was undertaken" are first and foremost to "promote the interests of humanity" (3–4). It may be inevitable that he will be compared to his fellow Africans and/or slaves, but that is not, this opening makes clear, the only possible nor Equiano's ideal identification.

The explicit subject of the remainder of the opening chapter will be the site of Equiano's most specific originating identity, the African nation of Benin into which he was born. In his initial description of both that nation and his childhood home within it, Equiano repeatedly stresses how isolated they were from the rest of the world. Benin, he notes, "runs back into the interior part of Africa, to a distance hitherto . . . unexplored by any traveler"; and he was born in "one of the most remote" of all that nation's provinces, so much so that while living there he had "never heard of white men or Europeans, nor of the sea." This isolation produced an extremely stable and static cultural identity, one that his individual narrative can entirely capture: "The manners and government of a people who have little commerce with other countries are generally very simple; and the history of what passes in one family or village, may serve as a specimen of the whole nation." Moreover, his family and identity were particularly tied to and representative of that village and nation: his ancestors, father, and brother all carried (both facially and linguistically) "the mark of grandeur" that signifies leadership, and Equiano too "was *destined* to receive it by my parents" (4–5). In that latter moment, which includes one of the chapter's only first-person singular pronouns, Equiano illustrates just how much his individual life and future overlapped at this earliest period of his life with those of his nation.

The chapter as a whole, however, is written in the present-day perspective from which Equiano narrates the entire book, and the two pronouns that he uses most frequently complicate that early identification on multiple levels. On the one hand, he uses the first-person plural a good deal, writing as an insider to his audience of (presumed) outsiders in order to provide a detailed description of this isolated place and culture. "We are almost a nation of dancers, musicians, and poets" (7), he notes in transitioning to a long paragraph on the culture's artistic productions and social structures, and both the "we" and the present tense serve there, as they do every time Equiano uses them, to bridge the gap between present and past identities and link him as directly to this community as did his destined mark. But just as frequently in this chapter Equiano separates those identities, creating instead the perspective of an experienced, eyewitness, but now outside ethnographer describing this culture. He does so in part through the use of third-person plural pronouns, as when he opens a paragraph on gender relationships with the sentence "Their mode of marriage is thus" (6). But even more telling of this ethnographic perspective are the many moments in which Equiano compares aspects of the Benin culture to other communities he has encountered in his travels: writing of a blue dye that is "brighter and richer than any I have seen in Europe"; noting that "they manufacture earthen vessels" to use as tobacco pipes "in the same manner as those in Turkey" (8); and so on. What these moments make especially clear, even at this opening moment in the narrative, is that Equiano has moved well beyond the isolated and static culture of his origin; that does not mean that he has not carried his first community with him to those new worlds, but neither can his perspective and identity remain unchanged by all the other communities that have influenced them. Exemplifying the multilayered perspective that results from that set of influences is the moment when Equiano first highlights a unique aspect of the Benin culture, the attributes that "give our dances a spirit and variety which I have scarcely seen elsewhere," but then includes a footnote in which he admits that "when I was in Smyrna I have frequently seen the Greeks dance after this manner" (7).

On one level, then, it is possible to read this opening chapter as Equiano's construction of his first, originating and still significant but also distinctly past, culture and identity. "Such is the imperfect sketch my memory has furnished me with of the manners and customs of the people among whom I first drew my breath" (19), he writes toward the chapter's end, and the sentence's complex combinations of both past and present tenses and first- and third-person pronouns reiterate the section's multiple perspectives while driving home the distance from which Equiano is creating his sketch. But he does not end the chapter with that sentence, and the striking historical frame with which he does conclude it introduces the possibility of a more cross-cultural identity even within this isolated original culture. At earlier moments in the chapter Equiano has seemed to argue that Benin's isolation is what gives the culture its strength, arguing that "the benefits of such a mode of living are obvious" and attributing more negative cultural traits like slaveholding to "those traders who brought the European goods . . . among us" (12–13). But in this concluding section, Equiano takes a significantly different perspective, arguing for "the strong analogy" between "the manners and customs of my countrymen" and "those of the Jews, before they reached the land of Promise." Far from attributing those similarities to simply ethnographic coincidence, Equiano notes that the "analogy alone would induce me to think that the one people had sprung from the other," and then goes on to highlight at length other potential arguments (from both his own experience and the works of other authors) for such a cross-cultural connection. And in case the rhetorical benefits of this connection are not obvious, Equiano ends the chapter with an impassioned plea to his European audience to remember that their ancestors "were once, like the Africans, uncivilized, and even barbarous. Did Nature make *them* inferior to their sons?" (19–22). Even if the Benin culture is part of the African past—and the chapter's formal choices and multilayered perspectives make clear that it is certainly part of Equiano's personal past—it can be, this almost typological analogy illustrates, a significantly seminal historical influence.

The comparison between the Benin and Jewish cultures is not the only such cross-cultural link that Equiano develops in his first chapter's closing pages. Just as he grounds his ethnographic descriptions in details gleaned from his many travels, so too does Equiano utilize evidence from other combinatory cultural communities—in both his old and new worlds—to emphasize the evolving and hybrid identities that these combinations can produce. "The Spaniards who have inhabited America under the torrid zone for any time," he notes, "are become as dark colored as our native Indians of Virginia, of which *I myself have been a witness*. There is another instance of a Portuguese settlement at Mitomba, a river in Sierra Leone, where the

inhabitants are bred from a mixture of the first Portuguese discover-
ers with the natives, and are now become, in their complexion, and
in the woolly quality of their hair, *perfect negroes*, retaining, however, a smattering of the Portuguese language" (21). The passage's
formal choices and ideas are, it is worth noting, as layered as the
identities about which Equiano is writing: from Equiano's own self-
positioning as a part of "Virginia" through the use of "our," but also
an outside "witness" to the increasingly interconnected European
and native cultures present in that new world; to the multiple elements, including skin color and complexion, hair quality, and language, that constitute and yet complicate "perfect" cultural identity.
Yet just as important as those specifics is the passage's overall portrayal of the transatlantic world in which Equiano will move for the
remainder of his life. It is a world defined, it seems, by an increasing difficulty of maintaining or distinguishing distinct cultures and
identities. And while it is a world created in part by slavery, it is also
the product of exploration, settlement, and above all movement and
cross-cultural encounter. Equiano notes in this opening chapter that
his given name, Olaudah, "signifies vicissitude, or fortunate also"
(16), and it is precisely the mutable nature of identity, foreshadowed
in the cross-cultural heritage he claims here for Benin, that charac-
terizes both the new world into which he will move and the very
fortunate life that he will ultimately find and create in it.

Equiano's initial vicissitudes of identity are, of course, produced
not by his will or by good fortune but rather by his kidnapping away
from his village and into a state of slavery, and it is on the multiple
stages of that process that chapter 2 entirely focuses. The chapter's
explicit events are thus profoundly painful ones for Equiano, as he
is wrenched away from his family and the entire world of his childhood; he transitions from the first chapter's distant but happy memories into this very distinct tone immediately, noting in the opening
paragraph that "I still look back with pleasure on the first scenes of
my life, though that pleasure has been for the most part mingled
with sorrow" (23). Exemplifying the loss of family and community that is the fullest source of such sorrow are Equiano's multiple
separations from his sister: they are kidnapped together but "soon
deprived of even the smallest comfort of weeping together" (25);
and they are subsequently reunited, only to have her "torn from me

for ever" the next morning. Equiano follows the latter tragedy by explicitly linking his sister to his foundational, lost but not forgotten cultural identity, apostrophizing directly to her: "Though you were early forced from my arms, your image has always been riveted in my heart, from which neither *time nor fortune* have been able to remove it." He ends the apostrophe by imagining the ways in which his sister might likewise have shifted from their original culture, but here those shifts are framed in direct relation to slavery's worst effects: "If your youth and delicacy have not long since fallen victims to the violence of the African trader, the pestilential stench of a Guinea ship, the seasoning in the European colonies, or the lash and lust of a brutal and unrelenting overseer" (30).

Yet concurrent with Equiano's own introduction to slavery's horrific realities throughout and beyond this chapter is his own first significant cultural shift, a move from the specific community of Benin to a broader, pan-African culture and perspective. That shift results partly from Equiano's recognition of how much he shares with cultures that he believed to be quite distant, literally and otherwise, from his originating one: he notes with surprise, shortly after the initial separation from his sister, that "although I was a great many days journey from my father's house, yet these people spoke exactly the same language with us" (25–26). That recognition, in turn, triggers the kind of instinctive cross-cultural response, an alignment of his own evolving identity with those of the encountered cultures, that will guide Equiano at each stage of his journeys. "From the time I left my own nation," he writes, "I always found somebody that understood me till I came to the sea coast. The languages of different nations did not totally differ, nor were they so copious as those of the Europeans, particularly the English. They were therefore easily learned; and, while I was journeying thus through Africa, I acquired two or three different tongues" (29). So well does Equiano embrace this broader African identity, in fact, that at one point he finds himself part of his (temporarily) adopted community's privileged slaveholding class, a shift that he explicitly connects to such cultural commonalities: the similarities, he admits, "made me forget that I was a slave. The language of these people resembled ours so nearly, that we understood each other perfectly. They had also the very same customs as we. There were likewise slaves daily to attend us" (30–31).

Equiano may be able to forget his condition in individual moments, however, but he is still very much a slave, and it is that role, and more precisely the initial encounters with European cultures that it produces, that solidifies his burgeoning African identity. When he is forced to leave the aforementioned privileged position, the next community to which he is brought foreshadows these more truly foreign cultural contacts: its "inhabitants . . . differed from us in all those particulars," including their use of "European cutlasses and cross bows, which were unknown to us" (32). Shortly thereafter he arrives at the coast and sees his first slave ship, and even more significantly its entirely culturally distinct crew: "Their complexions too differing so much from ours, their long hair, and the language they spoke, which was very different from any I had ever heard." Not coincidentally, Equiano's first glimpse of this culture is immediately followed by his recognition of the fundamental unity of the ship's seemingly diverse African captives, as he witnesses and then joins the "multitude of black people of every description chained together, every one of their countenances expressing dejection and sorrow." It is through conversation about this new and opposed culture that Equiano most explicitly joins the ship's Africans, asking "black people" about "those white men"; it is precisely the culture's thoroughly foreign nature that most interests him, as he wonders aloud "how comes it in all our country we never heard of them?" (34–35). Once the ship leaves Africa and begins the Middle Passage to the West Indies, both of these cultural definitions are reinforced for Equiano: his connection to the ship's Africans, since "in this situation I expect every hour to share the fate of my companions"; and the dependence of that connection on opposition to the whites, since "every circumstance I met with served only to render my state more painful, and heighten my apprehensions and my opinion of the cruelty of the whites" (37–38). And his shift to this African slave culture seems complete by both voyage's and chapter's end: Equiano the slave arrives at Barbados, where "there came to us Africans of all languages" and they are all sold at auction; and Equiano the narrator makes an impassioned protest against the slave trade by addressing "nominal Christians" as "an African" (40–42).

At the same time that his life and narrative are moving toward that African slave identity, however, Equiano provides glimpses into a more individual and mutable perspective and identity. In the midst of one of his most graphic descriptions of the Middle Passage's horrors, Equiano abruptly transitions to his initial encounters with both "flying fishes, which surprised [him] very much" and the quadrant, a technological innovation that provokes "astonishment" and "curiosity"; the latter response is "gratif[ied]" when one of the white seamen, no longer quite so thoroughly separate from Equiano, allows him "one day [to] look through" the navigational device. Despite the ship's ongoing terrors, Equiano notes that such events "heightened my wonder," and leave him "now more persuaded than ever that I [am] in another world, and that every thing about me [is] magic." Tellingly, the very next line is "At last, we came in sight of the island of Barbados," for Equiano's first experiences in the Americas will largely confirm his sense of wonder and magic: even in the "merchant's yard," where he and his fellow slaves are held pending their sales, "every object [is] new to" Equiano, and "every thing I [see] fill[s] me with surprise" and the renewed belief that "these people [are] full of nothing but magical arts" (39–41). When he is sold and transported to Virginia, this individual perspective and identity are only strengthened. Partly that is due to his isolation, as in this new setting he finds "not one soul who could talk to" him; the situation separates him from his fellow slaves, since they "could talk to each other, but I [have] no person to speak to that I [can] understand." But his surprised and wondering perspective likewise continues here, as he "indulges myself a great deal in looking about," and is rewarded by his first encounters with both a clock and a painting, further proof that "these people [are] all made of wonders" (43–45).

It is perhaps most accurate to say that as of this moment Equiano's identity is still entirely in development; he is, after all, only "near twelve years of age" (49), and so would be in the midst of his formative years even without such constant shifts. In the context of his almost immediate next such geographic shift—he is sold once more and bound for England—he notes that he is "still at a loss to conjecture my destiny" (45), and the phrase suggests both his identity fluctuations and his desire to play an active role in their evolution. On the surface, he has as a slave virtually no say in these shifts, as symbolized by his multiple renamings in these chapters: he writes that "in this place [Virginia] I was called Jacob; but on board the African scow I was called Michael," and when he is onboard the new ship his "captain and master name[s] me *Gustavus Vassa*"; he prefers to remain Jacob and "at first . . . refuse[s] to answer to my new name," but that only "gain[s] me many a cuff," and so he "submit[s]" and was known by Gustavus Vassa "ever since" (45–46). But in a subtle way he nonetheless expresses here his ability to influence, or at least respond actively to, the changes in his individual identity, as related on two levels to voice: by now he can "smatter a little imperfect English" and so "want[s] to know as well as I [can] where we [are] going"; and he imagines what his experiences and identity would mean if he were able to return home, "what wonders I should have to tell" to that foundational but much more static community (46).

While he is not destined to experience such a return, Equiano does form in the course of this next voyage a particularly meaningful and cross-cultural new community in his friendship with Richard Baker. Baker would seem to represent the white culture to which Equiano's African slave culture is on every level opposed: he is "a native of America," has "received an excellent education" there, and has even possessed "many slaves of his own." But more important than those distinctions are the two youth's shared experiences: Baker, only "four or five years older than" Equiano, has "never been at sea before," and he and Equiano go "through many sufferings together on shipboard, . . . many nights [lying] in each other's bosoms when we were in great distress." Those unifying experiences make Baker an excellent model for Equiano's evolving identity, one who is "of very great use to" Equiano as a "constant companion and instructor" over the "space" of his formative next "two years." That role is due in part to Baker's knowledge, his ability to serve as "a kind interpreter" between Equiano and this still very foreign English-speaking new world; but it is produced even more by Baker's status as a representative cross-cultural figure, one "who, at the age of fifteen," has "a mind superior to prejudice" and is thus "not ashamed to notice, to associate with, and to be the friend and instructor of, one who was ignorant, a stranger of a different complexion, and a slave!" (47).

It is through Baker's cross-cultural influence and inspiration that Equiano, after his arrival in England, attends church for the first time, develops his lifelong curiosity for and interest in books, and eventually enlists in the Royal Navy. All of those next steps in Equiano's evolving process of identity formation are due to his embrace of an open-minded perspective quite like Baker's: "I was so far from being afraid of any new thing which I saw," Equiano notes of his mindset during his first naval voyage, that "I even began to long for an engagement" (52–53), and the phrase reflects his desire for any and all experiences within this mobile and evolving cultural identity. And when he does encounter an extended naval battle in chapter 4, he entertains, significantly, "the hope, if I survive the battle, of relating it . . . when I should return," not to Africa, but instead "to London" (70).

As that shift in potential future audience implies, Equiano's evolving individual identity has by chapter 4 reached what seems to be a culmination. The chapter's opening paragraph highlights two explicit statements of ways in which his perspective is now that of a mobile Englishman, rather than an African slave.[6] Having spent "a great part" of his "three or four years" since arriving in England at sea, Equiano begins "to consider myself as happily situated" in that world; even more tellingly, "from the various scenes I had beheld on ship-board," he has become "a stranger to terror of every kind, and [is], in that respect, at least almost an Englishman." Moreover, having gained through that service the ability to "speak English tolerably well," Equiano can now call his shipmates "new countrymen," and can admit that he "no longer look[s] upon them as spirits, but as men superior to us; and therefore" that he has "the stronger desire to resemble them; to imbibe their spirit, and imitate their manners." Not only have his perspective and ideal identity shifted from African to English, but so too, more strikingly still, have his memories: where once they were consumed with images of his originating culture and family, now he notes that "every new thing that I observed I treasured up in my memory," as one more potential "occasion of improvement." As that emphasis on improvement suggests, Equiano has likewise shifted his perspective on his ideal future; he now emphasizes the possibility of a Christian afterlife, and thus asks his master for and to his "great joy" receives his baptism, "by my present name" of Gustavus Vassa. And as if to reinforce just how much this religious change connects to Equiano's New World identity, the clergyman who performs the service gives Equiano "at the same time" a book "called a guide to the Indians" (61–63).[7]

No shift in an individual's identity is ever as simple or absolute as a baptism might imply, of course, and the remainder of chapter 4 includes three brief but complex incidents that illustrate both the lingering presence of Equiano's African identities and his continuing evolution away from them. In the first, Equiano's ship arrives at Gibraltar and he tells some of its inhabitants "the story of my being kidnapped with my sister, and of our being separated"; his "heart leap[s] for joy" when he is told that his sister is being held nearby, but it turns out to be a woman "of another nation," albeit one who is "so like my sister that at first sight I really thought it was her" (64). Paralleling that moment's vision of potential but thwarted reconnection to his African past is "a trifling incident which surprise[s] [Equiano] agreeably" when he returns to England some time later. Another "black boy about my own size" sees Equiano and "transported at the sight of one of his own countrymen" runs "to meet me with the utmost haste." Equiano's reactions to this impassioned stranger are particularly complex: at first, "not knowing what [the boy is] about," he "turn[s] a little out of his way"; the boy's familial embrace, catching "hold of me in his arms as if I had been his brother," does lead them to a friendship in which they are "very happy in frequently seeing each other"; but when his ship receives its orders to "fit out . . . for another expedition," Equiano freely and with no regrets departs from his friend, noting that he "long[s] to engage in new adventures and see fresh wonders." Whereas the other boy seems to desire nothing more than to revisit the past, Equiano has, he admits, "a mind on which every thing uncommon made its full impression, and which consider[s] every event . . . as marvelous" (71).

It was due in large part to such a mutual open-minded perspective that Equiano had developed his more enduring friendship with Richard Baker. When he hears, shortly after the encounter with his false sister, of Baker's death, Equiano finds a way to receive his final possessions, which he "regard[s] as a memorial of my friend, whom I loved and grieved for as a brother" (65). A similar, even more intricate cross-cultural connection comprises the chapter's third incident. Equiano frames the moment as centrally connected to both levels of his communal African identity: the broader slave community, as he notes that he thinks "now of nothing but being freed, and working for" himself; and the specific Benin community, as he is "wonderfully surprised" to see in Biblical passages "the laws and rules of my own country written almost exactly [there]; a circumstance which I believe tended to impress our manners and customs more deeply on my memory." He is able to read those passages because of the instruction and explanations of Daniel Queen, an older sailor who becomes "like a father to" Equiano, so much so that "some even used to call [Equiano] after [Queen's] name." Equiano makes clear that Queen becomes central not only to his present identity and perspective—"Indeed I almost loved him with the affection of a son"—but also to his ideal future, as he now (with Queen's encouragement) connects the possibility of obtaining his freedom to a desire to be "instruct[ed] in [Queen's] business" and to "gain a good livelihood" alongside his mentor. And this new direction for his life and future, accompanied by the many other identity shifts that have taken place in this chapter, gives Equiano a new and stronger individual voice: at the close of the chapter a new master, Captain Doran, attempts to buy Equiano and he resists, telling Doran that he is "free," that he has "been baptized," and that "by the laws of the land no man has a right to sell" him. Doran's angry reply, that Equiano "talk[s] too much English," reflects how fully Equiano's evolving identity seems in this moment to differentiate him from the role of African slave (79–82).

Yet in that moment Equiano is still a slave, and despite his assertions he both recognizes Doran's present "power over" him and "recollect[s] . . . my former sufferings in the slave-ship" (82). The moment's results bear out those concerns, as Equiano's master hands him over to Doran, creating the literal and perspectival return to slavery in the West Indies with which chapter 5 begins: "Thus, at the moment I expected all my toils to end," Equiano writes in that chapter's first sentence, "was I plunged, as I supposed, in a new slavery, in comparison of which all my service hitherto had been perfect freedom; and whose horrors, always present to my mind, now rushed on it with tenfold aggravation" (83). Despite a professed if faint belief that "the *Lord would appear* for my deliverance" (84),

Equiano describes his return to this version of the Middle Passage as very much a reunification with the shipboard slave perspective: "I, a prisoner on board, now without hope!" As if to drive home how fully his identity in this place and moment once again aligns with those of all fellow slaves, he inserts in the text here a number of lines from "The Dying Negro," a 1773 poem in which the speaker describes being "dragg'd once more beyond the western main . . . where [his] poor countrymen in bondage wait / The long enfranchisement of a ling'ring fate" (86).[8] And the voyage ends with Equiano back in the West Indies, "the land of bondage," a place made even darker by both his own past experiences ("My former slavery now rose in dreadful review to my mind") and his recent and more ideal identity shifts ("I had been so long used to a European climate, that at first I felt the scorching West India sun very painful") (87–88).

Equiano spends much of the remainder of chapter 5 highlighting the many horrors of slave life in that West Indian land of bondage, and does so in a multilayered perspective similar to that through which he described Benin in chapter 1. The chapter's entire second half comprises a thorough accounting of "the cruelties of every kind, which were exercised on my unhappy fellow slaves" (94); Equiano not only goes to great lengths to highlight those instances to which he "was often a witness" while "employed by my master" (94) but also includes extensive statistics and historical contexts, through which to capture the slave system more generally. Moreover, as he did with his village in Benin, Equiano argues explicitly that the commonalities across the slave community more than outweigh any specific distinctions, and thus that "the history of an island, or a plantation, with a few such exceptions . . . might serve for a history of the whole" (103). He likewise goes to great pains to differentiate the islands' slave community from its white one, arguing that one reason for the length of this section is that "some people [have] been hardy enough of late to assert, that negroes are on the same footing [in the West Indies] as Europeans" (101). And he ends with an extended apostrophe to the slaveholders in his audience on behalf of "us enslav'd," imploring them to "change your conduct, and treat your slaves as men" (105). After all, whatever the specifics of his experiences and identity, Equiano recognizes that he is on a broad level entirely implicated in the islands' system of slavery; he concludes a paragraph detailing the "melancholy tales" of "a poor Creole negro I knew well" by noting that "even this poor man and I should some time after suffer together in the same manner" (102–3).

Yet Equiano's position in and perspective on slavery are significantly more complex than that, both in the present moment being described in the chapter and in the future toward which he occasionally and crucially gestures here. In the present, the reason why Equiano is generally a witness to, rather than the subject of, the cruelties he describes is that he has been purchased by Robert King, a Quaker merchant from Philadelphia who recognizes the unique qualities of Equiano's identity and experiences (partly his "good character," but mostly the knowledge and skills he has "learned on ship board") and makes clear that he does "not mean to treat [Equiano] as a common slave" (89–90). King is as good as his word, as Equiano details through an extended comparison with "a countryman of mine" who receives much harsher treatment; and the broader contrast between "the dreadful usage of the poor men" in the islands and Equiano's own "situation" drives home his arguments that he still has "all the opportunity I could wish for" (91–93). Even more telling is Equiano's one explicit reference, in the midst of an extended argument about more and less humane and productive methods for managing slave plantations, to a striking future opportunity and role; he cites a "gentleman" who "has written a treatise on the usage of his own slaves" in order to substantiate his arguments, and then includes this seeming aside: "I myself, as shall appear in the sequel, managed an estate, where, by those attentions, the negroes were uncommonly cheerful and healthy, and did more work by half than by the common mode of treatment they usually do" (96–97). Whatever the present parallels between his identity and the slave community more generally, this astonishing sentence leaves no doubt that his individual identity remains destined for a significantly distinct (and, to a modern reader, troubling, on which more below) future.

The opening of chapter 6 makes clear that it is the continued development of that individual identity on which the remainder of the narrative will focus. Arguing that "the punishments of the slaves" and "the different instruments with which they are tortured" are both "so well known" and yet "too shocking to yield delight either to the writer or the reader," Equiano pledges to "hereafter only mention such as incidentally befell myself in the course of my adventures" (106). "Incidentally" is the sentence's crucial word, for while Equiano's official identity will remain that of a slave for some time, and so his experiences continue to comprise "slaving, as it were for life, sometimes at one thing, and sometimes at another" (108), the specifics of his existence virtually elide that identity's meaning. "I received better treatment from [King] than any other I believe ever met with in the West Indies in my situation," Equiano admits, and he once again takes full advantage of the opportunities presented by such treatment, "endeavor[ing] to try my luck, and commence merchant[ing]" (109–10). He certainly pursues that new career in direct response to both his slave status and the broader realities of African existence in the Americas; for example, upon witnessing "a new scene of horror," the "dreadful . . . state of a free negro" in the world of slavery, Equiano reiterates his commitment to do whatever he can "to obtain my freedom, and to return to Old England" (117). But the financial independence that his merchant career provides allows Equiano to continue developing his more fully individual identity, one very much connected to Christianity (he buys a Bible and notes that it and his baptismal gift, "the Guide to the Indians," are "the two books I loved above all others" [113]) and just as clearly distinguished from the identities of his fellow Africans (he is "obliged to hire some black men to help me pull a boat across the water to go in quest of" a white South Carolina merchant who has cheated him [125]; later he notes without comment that his ship takes "in a live cargo, . . . as we call a cargo of slaves" [130]).

The best example of Equiano's prioritizing of his individual over his slave identity in this section of the narrative comes with his manumission in chapter 7. That event is the direct result of Equiano's merchant activities and the strengthened will and voice they have helped him find, as evidenced by the extended debate in which Equiano (along with his "true friend, the captain") convinces his master to "let him have his freedom" (133). Equiano certainly highlights the event's singular significance, noting with amazement how "before night, I who had been a slave in the morning, trembling at the will of another, now became my own master, and completely free," and calling it "the happiest day I had ever experienced" (135). And he depicts the monumental change in identity that his manumission produces, highlighting how "the fair as well as the black people immediately styled me by a new appellation, to me the most desirable in the world, which was freeman" (136). Yet his narrative's structure belies those emphases somewhat, as he does not end the chapter with the manumission; instead, he concludes by detailing at length a subsequent and more individual experience and identity shift, the voyage on which his captain dies and Equiano "now obtain[s] a new appellation, . . . captain." He admits that "this elate[s] me not a little," as it is "quite flattering to my vanity to be thus styled by as high a title as any sable freeman in this place possessed" (143–44). While it would be possible (if difficult) for any slave to gain the title of freeman, Equiano's nautical role and successes seem much more unique and individual to him, and I believe it is profoundly telling that it is on those elements that he both ends chapter 7 and focuses all of chapter 8. In the latter he averts a disastrous shipwreck and so can "not help looking on myself as the principal instrument in effecting our deliverance" and as "a kind of chieftain amongst them" (151–52).

It is precisely the connection between his nautical role and his ideal identity that produces Equiano's desire to continue moving, a desire that motivates his choices throughout the next few chapters. He recognizes the possibility of developing his individual identity within the New World, or at least within particularly cross-cultural communities therein: New Providence in the Bahamas, which includes a number of "free black people . . . who [are] very happy" and which Equiano "like[s] extremely" (159); and St. Pierre on Martinique, a city that is "built more like a European town than any I had seen in the West Indies" and where, being "much respected by all the gentleman in the place," Equiano could stay and "in a short time have land and slaves of my own" (163–66). But he continually encounters the limitations of his African identity in the New World, finding in Georgia that he "talk[s] too good English" for the locals (161) and on Martinique that he "should be compelled to submit to [the] degrading necessity, which every black freeman is under, of advertising himself like a slave, when he leaves an island" (165). It is for these reasons that he decides to "take a final farewell of the American quarter of the globe" (161) and return to England, although before he does so he experiences one particularly complex final encounter with a "black woman" in Georgia. The woman's child has died, "and not able to get any white person to perform" the "burial service," she asks Equiano to do so; he initially resists but "at last consent[s] to act the parson for the first time in my life. As she [is] much respected, there [is] a great company both of white and black people at the grave. I then accordingly assumed my new vocation, and performed the funeral ceremony to the satisfaction of all present; after which I bid adieu to Georgia" (162). As this moment illustrates, wherever Equiano travels he will on the one hand be included in and thus remain connected to the broader African community, while on the other hand his ability to acquire new vocations and satisfy multiple communities will allow for continued development of his individual identity.

That individual identity, importantly, does not quite fit with the community of London, to which Equiano sails after leaving the Americas. He believes that in undertaking that voyage he is "steering the course I had long wished for," and at the journey's conclusion his "longing eyes" are "once more gratified with a sight of London, . . . a scene quite new to me, but full of hope" (167). Yet while he does continue to grow there, improving "in arithmetic" and learning the French horn (a skill that will provide him with another career in his later years), in a very short time he determines "to try the sea again, . . . as I had been bred to it, and had hitherto found the profession of it successful" (169). Not only has sailing been a profession for Equiano; it also matches well with what he admits is his "roving disposition," his "desire [to] see as many different parts of the world as" he can (175). That desire parallels the outsider's, ethnographic perspective that Equiano has taken on each of his earlier communities in the text, from the originating one of Benin to that of slavery in the West Indies. And in the voyages he undertakes after leaving London he falls easily and comfortably into that perspective once again: remarking on "the richness and beauty of the countries" he visits, "and struck with the elegant buildings with which they abound" (170); pursuing his desire to "see the different modes of worship of the people wherever" he goes (173); and so on. He is just as much of an outsider to the slave and/or African cultures that he encounters on these travels, and is thus able to observe and judge them objectively: he criticizes the "truly piteous and wretched" condition of the "galley-slaves" in Italy, a situation that "disgrace[s]" the place's "grandeur" (172); and even when he returns to the West Indies he retains this outsider's perspective, noting with "surprise . . . the number of Africans assembled together" in Kingston (Jamaica) and describing how "each different nation of Africa meet and dance, after the manner of their own country" and "their native customs" (176). From his sailor's perspective, Africans in Jamaica or galley slaves in Italy are both interesting elements of the local communities, cultures to be observed and then moved beyond, in search of the next destination; exemplifying this role's constant movement and discovery is the voyage to the North Pole with which Equiano ends chapter 9, a journey that takes his ship "farther, by all accounts, than any navigator had even ventured before" (182).

If the North Pole provides an excellent symbol for the lengths to which Equiano is willing to go in pursuit of his individual identity, he likewise returns to and makes even more central in these chapters an ongoing spiritual voyage: his increasing "determin[ation] to work out my own salvation, and, in so doing, procure a title to Heaven." His "own salvation" is precisely accurate, as Equiano views this Christian journey as both deeply individual and tied to no specific community: he is "determined (in my own strength) to be a first-rate Christian," and is willing to "join . . . whatever sect or party I [find] adhering" to his understanding of scripture (183–84). Once again this individual identity takes him beyond any one place, and so he "resolve[s], at that time, never more to return to England" (187), setting sail once again in search of "Christian fellowship" wherever he can find it (190). Tellingly, his best model for that kind of spiritual journey is found in another personal narrative, "a little book entitled 'The Conversion of an Indian'"; the work narrates the life of a "poor man" who comes "over the sea . . . to enquire after the Christian's God" and has "not his journey in vain" (192). For Equiano too his spiritual journey is paralleled, and in fact greatly supported, by his literal travels, and it is thus during a "delightful voyage to Cadiz" that Equiano takes advantage of his "many opportunities of reading the Scriptures" and reaches his spiritual epiphany (196–97). And in the "Miscellaneous Verses; or, Reflections on the State of [his] Mind" that Equiano inserts into his text between that epiphany and the book's final two chapters, he explicitly connects that spiritual journey to his "orphan state"; initially he "had to mourn" that lack of a stable community and his resulting "forsaken" and "forlorn" identity, but it is ultimately his inability to remain in either "the place that gave me birth" or "the English nation" that allows him to find his individual salvation (202–7).

Moreover, having achieved that individual goal, Equiano can begin to occupy and even create new, explicitly cross-cultural communal roles. The first opportunity for such a role is offered to Equiano by a Spanish priest who "solicits" Equiano to "go to one of the universities in Spain," and argues that if he becomes a priest himself, he "might in time become even a Pope," since "Pope Benedict was a black man." Equiano, not being a Catholic, resists this "temptation," but he does acknowledge that it matches well with a nature "ever desirous of learning" and of converting others to his faith (210–11). His nature is also of course that of a captain, and his next opportunity allows him to exercise all of these elements of his individual identity. His current employer, Dr. Irving, has "a mind for a new adventure, . . . cultivating a plantation at Jamaica," and he asks Equiano to accompany him; explicitly Equiano will manage "his estate," but implicitly it also represents a chance for him "to be an instrument . . . of bringing some poor sinner to my well-beloved master, Jesus Christ" (213). He performs both of those roles in particularly complex and cross-cultural ways: on the voyage to the New World he sails with "four Musquito Indians, . . . chiefs in their own country" and "in [the] passage I took all the pains that I could to instruct the Indian prince in the doctrines of Christianity, of which he was entirely ignorant" (213–14); and his first act as Irving's manager is "to purchase some slaves to carry with us, and cultivate a plantation; and I chose them all of my own countrymen" (216). In many ways Equiano's actions and perspective in this latter role reinforce the most unsettling aspects of his earlier aside about managing slaves—he uses the labor of the local "unenlightened Indians . . . exactly like [that of] the Africans" (218); and he even staves off a native insurrection using his education, "recollecting a passage I had read in the Life of Columbus" and "frightening" the locals "by telling them of certain events in the heavens" (220). It would be entirely possible to analyze Equiano's individual identity here, with its combination of Christian missionary and plantation overseer, as simply representative of

the European system of slavery, exploitation, and forced conversion
that has in many respects defined the New World since the era of
Cabeza de Vaca.

Equiano goes to significant lengths here, however, to indicate
some of the complexities in his relationship to and perspective on
this New World plantation community and its various cultures.
He admits that there "was not one white person in our dwelling,
nor any where else . . . that was better or more pious than those
unenlightened Indians" (218); and later, when he is taken captive
by unscrupulous Europeans, he is saved by another group of natives
who "act towards me more like Christians than those whites I was
amongst" (227). Even more crucially, he develops a communal connection with the plantation's African slaves, so much so that when
he decides to return to his seafaring lifestyle and asks Irving for his
discharge, "all my poor countrymen, the slaves, when they heard of
my leaving them, were very sorry, as I had always treated them with
care and affection, and did every thing I could to comfort the poor
creatures, and render their condition easy" (223–24). And he explicitly contrasts that community with the much more hierarchical and
negative one that replaces it: he hears some time later that "after I
had left the estate, . . . a white overseer had supplied my place: this
man, through inhumanity and ill-judged avarice, beat and cut the
poor slaves most unmercifully," leading to the plantation's failure
(232). Given that slavery and its parallel social systems comprised a
central and unavoidable part of pan-American culture in this Revolutionary era, it is perhaps more accurate to analyze Equiano's new
identity and roles as mitigating, rather than contributing to, their
effects and existence.

It is precisely in that light that the various social and political activities on which Equiano's final chapter focuses can best be
understood. For example, when Equiano decides to pursue a career
as "a missionary to Africa," he argues in a letter to the Bishop of London that his cross-cultural experiences and identity as "a native of
Africa," who "has resided in different parts of Europe for twenty-two
years" but who remains "acquainted with the language and customs
of the country," uniquely qualify him for the role (235–36). More
multipartite but still directly related to his cross-cultural identity are
Equiano's contributions to efforts like the proposed recolonization

"expedition to Sierra Leone," one that will "send the Africans from hence to their native quarter" (241); or the "petition on behalf of my African brethren" in which he implores the Queen to abolish the slave trade (248–49); or his extended arguments for British colonization of Africa, in order to extend the benefits of "civilization" to "the native inhabitants" (250–53). Of these various causes, only the abolitionist one is likely to strike a modern reader as entirely savory, with each of the others seeming to indicate the distance that Equiano has traveled from both his specific and broad African communal origins. Yet each can also represent the kind of cross-cultural movement and community that has produced Equiano's individual identity and provided his most ideal culture. And he likewise highlights an exemplary such community in his final chapter, narrating a 1785 trip to his "favorite old town" of Philadelphia, and remarking with great pleasure on the "free-school the worthy Quakers had erected for every denomination of black people, whose minds are cultivated here, and forwarded to virtue; and thus they are made useful members of the community." Equiano even "present[s] [an] address" to the city's Quakers, thanking them on behalf of "we, part of the poor, oppressed, needy, and much degraded negroes" for working to create this new kind of egalitarian, post-Revolution American community (239–40).

As progressive as that community is, however, it is still largely defined by African and European cultural presences, with the latter certainly working to improve the former's condition but with an ongoing and clear distinction in identity and power between the two cultures (as evidenced by both Equiano's immediate connection to that "we" and his recognition of how dependant those negroes are on their audience's efforts and mercy). And so it is with another, more truly revolutionary New World community that I would end this analysis of Equiano's identity shifts. During his time as Irving's plantation manager, Equiano takes part in a lengthy celebration, one organized by the Musquito tribe; he initially finds the event's plans and details entirely foreign to his sensibilities and goes "home not a little disgusted at the preparations." But when the event starts, such boundaries are explicitly and fully crossed time and again, such as the moment in which Dr. Irving "join[s] the males" (both native and African) in their dances. Equiano describes the festivities at great length, partly as an outside ethnographer (describing for example the texture and smell of "a raw piece of alligator") and partly in relation to his African countrymen (he notes that "our people skipped amongst [the natives] out of complaisance"). And he ends the paragraph by celebrating the event itself, noting that "this merry-making at last ended without the least discord in any person in the company, although it was made up of different nations and complexions" (221–22).

Equiano concludes his narrative by returning to the metatextual perspective with which he began it, hoping that the reader's "censure will be suspended" despite his stylistic "plainness of truth" in detailing his life's events. That "life and fortune," he admits, "have been extremely checkered, and my adventures various." Yet they have all contributed significantly to his identity, with "every event in my life [making] an impression on my mind, and influenc[ing] my conduct." And his final wish is that his identity and text will likewise "afford some profit" to "those who are possessed of this spirit," who are willing to learn from all the fortunate vicissitudes he has experienced (254). In many ways, the American Revolution and the national identity and narratives created there would seem to depend on eliding lives and identities like Equiano's, or at least on refining them into the nation's community in the process implied by Wheatley's "On Being Brought."[9] Yet both the African origins and the subsequent cross-cultural experiences and perspectives that constitute Wheatley and Equiano's identities are in fact themselves revolutionary American identities, mobile and evolving lives that exemplify what distinguished this New World community and comprised the strongest arguments for its independence and future.

Transformative Expansions

Sarah Winnemucca's
Ideal Interpretations

In the preface to his culminating masterwork, *Ancient Society; or, Researches in the Lines of Human Progress from Savagery through Barbarism to Civilization* (1877), pioneering American anthropologist Lewis Henry Morgan articulates one of that text's and his career's principal goals: to determine "why other tribes and nations have been left behind in the race of progress." To answer that question, Morgan developed the theory of cultural evolution, an argument that cultures progress through the three stages indicated in the book's subtitle. As the word "other" implies, Morgan views the Native American tribes and nations on which his text focuses as distinctly outside of mainstream American culture; but he concurrently sees them as illustrative of an earlier stage in that culture, arguing in the preface that "the history and experience of American Indian tribes represent . . . the history and experience of our own remote ancestors when in corresponding conditions." Motivated by that sense of his subject's national and contemporary relevance as well as by his own anthropological methodology, Morgan is in *Ancient Society* as thorough and nuanced in his descriptions and analyses of Native American cultures as he was throughout his career; but his theory and perspective on those cultures nonetheless provide perfect corollaries to contemporary visions of Native Americans as a vanishing people. "The ethnic life of the Indian tribes is declining under the influence of American civilization," Morgan claims in support of his project's timeliness, locating his subjects very much in the nation's past; an understanding of their cultures might be crucial to a sense of America's present and future progress and civilization, as Morgan defines them, but there is precious little room within his implicit conception of that nation for Native Americans' ongoing presence and cultures.

If Morgan's publications built toward that argument about Native Americans' influential but vanishing presence, however, his experiences posed significant complications to that theory. He developed at a young age and maintained throughout his life a strong connection to the Seneca Iroquois tribe, and in his parallel careers as a lawyer and politician consistently fought for that tribe's present survival and future rights; Morgan in fact first ran for the New York State Senate in 1860 in order to fight the Ogden Land Company on behalf of the tribe's decades-long (and losing) effort to maintain tribal lands and sovereignty. Moreover, his relationship to the Seneca went well beyond that of an outside activist, as he was adopted into the tribe and became lifelong friends with Ely Parker, a Seneca chief who served as an engineer on the Erie Canal and a Union officer in the Civil War (among his many cross-cultural experiences). It was in direct collaboration with Parker—based, as he wrote in the book's dedication, on the two men's "joint researches" (vii)—that Morgan wrote his *League of the Ho-De-No-Sau-Nee or Iroquois* (1851), a seminal work of anthropology in which his subject is studied not for its historical relevance or illustration, but for its own present cultural identity and existence. As Morgan notes in that text's preface, such an understanding of the Seneca can be a first step toward a goal of "finally rais[ing them] to the position of citizens of the State"; but that goal will concurrently require all Americans to move away from their own cultural perspectives and prejudices. "The time has come," Morgan argues, "in which it is befitting to cast aside all ancient antipathies, all inherited opinions"; he positions himself as the perfect proponent for such a perspectival shift, due to his "adoption as a Seneca" (ix–xi). And his Seneca name, *Tayadaowuhkuh* ("bridging the gap"), thus signifies not only Morgan's efforts and ability to shift his individual perspective and identity but also his argument for a concurrent expansion of definitions of America, one not historically illustrated by, but inclusive of and interconnected with these very present cultures.

The national expansions that in many ways constituted American identity in the nineteenth century—from the geographic expansion of the Louisiana Purchase with which the century opened, to the imperialist endeavors and wars with which it closed—seemed to depend, as scholars such as John Dippel and Mark Rifkin have recently argued, upon an understanding of native and non-European cultures as precisely other, historical, and vanishing in the ways illustrated by Morgan's theory of cultural evolution. If the cultures did not acquiesce to their erasure, it was necessary for America to overcome them in order to expand; as the Columbian Exposition's national committee chairman (J. T. Harris) succinctly articulated that perspective in the fair's opening speech, "It remained for the Saxon race to people this new land, to redeem it from barbarism, . . . and in less than four centuries to make it the most powerful and prosperous country on which God's sunshine falls."[1] But geographic and imperialist expansions are not the only ones on which an analysis of nineteenth-century America can focus; many of the significant social changes in the century's latter half, from abolition to the waves of immigration from Eastern Europe and Asia, can likewise be read as opportunities to expand the definition of American identity. While the social changes pertaining to Native Americans in the era were largely limiting and destructive, as exemplified by the rise of the reservation system, both Morgan's experiences with the Seneca and his friend Ely Parker's cross-cultural life highlight how much native cultures remained a part of this expanding America. Moreover, the life and narrative of Morgan and Parker's contemporary Sarah Winnemucca illustrate just how fully Native Americans themselves had both struggled for generations and continued to grapple with these questions of identity and perspective, with what their relationship to European Americans specifically and America more broadly was and could be.

In many ways Winnemucca overtly represents her Paiute tribe, both as the daughter and granddaughter of chiefs and as a lifelong spokesperson for her people; much of the early scholarship on both Winnemucca and her text, from Sally Zanjani's biographical account of her role "as the eloquent voice of the Paiutes" (2–3) to

Siobhan Senier's tracing of "how [Winnemucca] worked to represent the Paiutes and herself to white audiences who made conflicting demands on her" (xii), focused on this explicitly native and relatively stable identity. Yet recent scholars have foregrounded instead Winnemucca's cultural and textual hybridity, her location of self and narrative in conversation with both the Paiute and European (among other) American cultures; illustrating this trend is Lorena Carbonera's extension of Mary Louise Pratt's concept of the "contact zone" to native autobiographers such as Winnemucca and their roles as "cultural mediators" (129).[2] Indeed, throughout her life and narrative Winnemucca becomes and positions herself as a mediating figure between the communities, developing a cross-cultural identity that unquestionably limits and pains her but also gives her the opportunity to imagine, give voice to, and work toward a more cross-cultural American identity and future.[3]

Even the title of Winnemucca's narrative, *Life Among the Piutes: Their Wrongs and Claims* (1883), reflects on multiple levels her complex and ambiguous relationship to her originating culture and identity. For one thing, the main title is almost certainly an allusion to a popular recent work of Euro-American autoethnography, Joaquin Miller's *Life Amongst the Modocs* (1873). Miller, one of the era's most prominent western Americans and authors, was a complicated cross-cultural figure in his own right, a man who participated in the California Gold Rush, took the pseudonym Joaquin from Joaquin Murietta (a notorious bandit and also the subject of the first Native American novel), and published his *Life* to capitalize on a controversial and disputed adoption into the California Modoc tribe, but who also worked and wrote for many years on behalf of that tribe and Native American rights more generally. Winnemucca's subtitle makes clear how much her book will likewise advocate for the experiences and voices of her tribe, at least as much as it will narrate her own life within that community. And while the word "among" might allude to Miller's title, it and the even more surprising "their" together also foreshadow Winnemucca's conflicted presence in that community, and the ways in which her role as an interpreter between her tribe and European American settlers, military officers, and government officials will provide her with the strongest means through which to advocate for their wrongs and claims, yet lead her own life experiences into an increasingly mediating and cross-cultural identity and perspective.

The book's one-page editor's preface, written by reformer Mary Mann, largely defines Winnemucca's identity and text in direct relation to her Native American culture and in contrast to Mann's and the audience's European American one. The book is, Mann argues, a "heroic act on the part of the writer" because of Winnemucca's "courageous purpose of telling in detail to the mass of our people ... the story of her people's trials." Moreover, she admits the text's "literary deficiencies" and connects them to Winnemucca's "own original words," words that, despite her editorial revisions for "correct orthography and punctuation," she is "confident that no one would desire ... should be altered." After all, Mann claims, the text is both a unique cultural artifact, "the first outbreak of the American Indian in human literature," and a compelling historical and political statement, since "at this moment, when the United States seem waking up to their duty to the original possessors of our immense territory, it is of the first importance to hear what only an Indian and an Indian woman can tell." Despite the present and future hope implied in that latter passage, Mann's distinction between the original possessors and our immense territory could allow for definitions of Winnemucca as embodying the noble and influential but vanishing Native Americans in an era of European American expansion. Her preface's final sentence, and especially its image of Winnemucca's familial past and role, seems to link her to precisely such an elegiac sentiment, noting of the book's narrative that "to tell it was her own deep impulse, and the dying charge given her by her father, the truly paternal chief of his beloved tribe" (4).

Mann's connection of the book not only to that lost past but also to Winnemucca's own impulse, and thus to her individual identity and perspective, is, however, a profoundly significant one. And her preface likewise hints, in two very telling phrases, at the cross-cultural experiences and identity that complicate any absolute connection of Winnemucca to her family and tribe. For one thing, Mann contrasts the text's literary deficiencies not only to her editorial knowledge of standard punctuation but also, and more immediately, to "the fervid eloquence which [Winnemucca's] extraordinary colloquial command of the English language enables her to utter" (4). While images of Native Americans as eloquent orators had been part of American life at least since Thomas Jefferson's famous passage on Chief Logan in *Notes on the State of Virginia* (1782),[4] Mann's emphasis on Winnemucca's command of English is nonetheless striking; this is a woman, as the second sentence of her narrative will highlight, who was already alive when her tribe encountered white settlers for the first time, rather than (for example) a mixed-race author such as William Apess, whose Pequot ancestors had interacted with Europeans for centuries. Yet despite that very recent history, Winnemucca has engaged with this new culture sufficiently to master its spoken language. Moreover, in the second striking passage Mann identifies a "single aim" for Winnemucca's text that is broader than narrating her people's trials: "*to tell the truth* as it lies in the heart and mind of a true patriot, and one whose knowledge of the two races gives her an opportunity of comparing them justly" (4). While "patriot" is an ambiguous term, and could describe Winnemucca's allegiance to her people, I would contend that, following as it does Mann's use of "American Indian" and directly preceding her reference to the "duty" of "the United States," it reads as more national than tribal in connotation. And without question the sentence's final clause locates Winnemucca as a national and mediating figure, one with a perspective and identity that straddle both Native and European American communities and with a text that will similarly direct its interpretations in both directions.

That text's dense opening paragraph foregrounds to what extent Winnemucca's individual identity is linked both to her tribe and outside of European American culture, while still introducing the cross-cultural complexities within and between those communities, and it is worth quoting in full:

I was born somewhere near 1844, but am not sure of the precise time. I was a very small child when the first white people came into our country. They came like a lion, yes, like a roaring lion, and have continued so ever since, and I have never forgotten their first coming. My people were scattered at that time over nearly all the territory now known as Nevada. My grandfather was chief of the entire Piute nation, and was camped near Humboldt Lake, with a small portion of his tribe, when a party traveling eastward from California was seen coming. When the news was brought to my grandfather, he asked what they looked like? When told that they had hair on their faces, and were white, he jumped up and clasped his hands together, and cried aloud,—"My white brothers,—my long-looked for white brothers have come at last!" (5)

Winnemucca does begin with the classic autobiographical "I was born," although even there the lack of an exact date implicitly locates her individual birth within a broader cultural worldview and perspective. The next sentence immediately shifts to both that cultural identity ("our country") and the contrasting and opposed culture ("the first white people"), and to the first contacts on which the entire chapter will focus (as illustrated by the chapter's title, "First Meeting of Piutes and Whites"). The multiple time periods introduced in the paragraph imply both the shifting geographic realities and the consistent cultural identities that will comprise the subjects of the subsequent chapters: the location of her people "at that time" foreshadowing the relocations and reservation system; the white people's "continued" forceful presence; and Winnemucca's inability to forget their arrival foreshadowing the fundamental division in the tribe's experiences and worlds before and after this exact historical moment. And even the profoundly communal identity of Winnemucca's grandfather, chief of this "entire" expansive "nation," seems to illustrate how much her individual life and experiences will represent these broader categories and cultures.

Yet it is precisely through this opening paragraph's introduction of her grandfather that Winnemucca foreshadows the cross-cultural complexities. For one thing, her grandfather notices the explicit physical differences between the arriving people and his tribal members (facial hair, skin color) but then immediately bridges the gap comprised by those differences through his repeated phrase "my white brothers." Moreover, he frames the whites' arrival, through the striking adjective "long-looked for," not as a moment of shift or even initial contact, but rather as the culmination of a historical narrative, the validation of a perspective that he has clearly held for some time. He more overtly expresses that perspective, and makes it explicitly communal as well, shortly thereafter, "summon[ing] his whole people" and sharing with them what Winnemucca calls a "tradition," an origin story that includes two dark and two white children within "a happy family in this world." While the story does include foundational "quarreling" between those children that leads "the father and mother" to "separate their children . . . across the mighty ocean," it explicitly frames the separation as temporary, to be ended by cross-cultural contact and reconnection: "The nation that sprung from the white children will some time send some one to meet us and heal all the old trouble." And Winnemucca's grandfather ends his oration by shifting explicitly from the mythic past to the historical present and future, claiming to his tribal audience that "they will come again, and I want you one and all to promise that, should I not live to welcome them myself, you will not hurt a hair on their heads, but welcome them as I tried to do" (6–7).

Winnemucca's own past experiences and present (1883) perspective do not allow her to end the moment on that note, and she follows the story both by recognizing "how good of" her grandfather it was "to try and heal the wound" and by bemoaning "how vain were his efforts!" (7). Yet she also devotes a significant portion of this opening chapter, one of the narrative's longest, to her grandfather's subsequent experiences and relationship with the arriving white settlers and military, all of which reinforce in his perspective his cross-cultural tradition's themes and hopes. For example, there is the humorous but also deeply symbolic culminating encounter between her grandfather and the whites who constitute the first "great emigration" to the area: her grandfather has made it a point to "call upon them" and "all [shake] hands," and when the "white brothers were going away they gave my grandfather a white tin plate"; he immediately makes it part of both his communal and individual identities, sharing it with "all his people" and then "bor[ing] holes in it and fasten[ing] it on his head, and [wearing] it as a hat." While the latter detail could be read as an illustration of Native Americans' lack of civilization or sophistication, Winnemucca follows it with a cross-cultural analogy that deflates such rigid cultural readings, noting that her grandfather "held [the hat] in as much admiration as my white sisters hold their diamond rings or a sealskin jacket" (7–8). Just as her grandfather is thus likened to whites and their silly but significant cultural practices, so too does Winnemucca's use of the phrase "white sisters" here tie her both to a potential white audience and to her grandfather's cross-cultural perspective on the human family.

When the next emigrants arrive the following year, her grandfather extends and deepens the connections between his identity and experiences and their presence. First, the group's leader, Captain Fremont, gives her grandfather a new name, Captain Truckee (Paiute for "all right" or "very well"), once again contributing a gift to his evolving cross-cultural identity (9). More meaningfully still, her grandfather and 11 other Paiutes depart for California with Fremont to fight for the United States in the Mexican War; when they return, they bring not only a variety of gifts and items from their fellow soldiers but also a new cross-cultural voice: "They spoke to their people in the English language, which was very strange to them all" (10). Through such experiences, her grandfather not only validates his vision of a historically united human family but also explicitly connects both his perspective and his community to those of the expanding United States. Ever the storyteller, he narrates to the tribe the "wonderful things" he has seen and done in California, and his performances include "sing[ing] . . . the air to the Star-spangled Banner, which everybody learn[s] during the winter" (18). And in a small but telling moment, Winnemucca makes clear that her grandfather's emphases on cross-cultural equality and family truly embody America's founding ideals: while the tribe is traveling with one group of settlers, her grandfather witnesses "the captain of the train . . . whipping negroes who were driving his team," and the mistreatment makes him "feel very badly" and declare "to his people that he would not travel with his white brothers any farther" (23–24). From her grandfather's perspective all men are indeed his brothers, equal and valued members of the human family whose long overdue reunion he is happily witnessing and helping shape in these years after initial contact.

Winnemucca is not her grandfather, however, and this opening chapter also traces the effects of these initial cultural encounters on her own, very young but complex and evolving perspective and identity. Many of her responses are driven by the uncertainty and fear that are the logical results of an encounter with an entirely unfamiliar people at a young age, particularly given the horrific rumors that circulate through the tribe about this distinct culture. Winnemucca recounts "a fearful story they told us children" during the period following initial contact, and it is not a lone voice passing along such stories: their "mothers told us that the whites were killing everybody and eating them, so we were all afraid of them"

(11). Moreover, these horror stories are accompanied in at least one instance by an action on the part of Winnemucca's family that is even more frightening and scarring for the young girl: hearing that "white people [are] coming" and fearful that they "shall all be killed and eaten up," her mother and aunt bury her and her cousin up to their necks, planting bushes over their faces and leaving them there "all day." As Winnemucca frames it, this premature burial combines with her cultural fear to produce the greatest possible discomfort: "Oh, can any one imagine my feelings *buried alive,* thinking every minute that I was to be unburied and eaten up by the people that my grandfather loved so much?" (11–12). Even in this extreme situation she remembers her grandfather's cross-cultural perspective, but the more explicitly and fearfully cultural views of both her mother's generation and her own young one are dominant in this moment. And the result is as metaphorical as it is painfully real, with Winnemucca left buried by these fears, entirely deprived of the mobility and will that are fundamental to her grandfather's hopes for cross-cultural relationships and progress. Nor, it is important to add, are Native American fears and actions the only nor the primary causes of that cultural stasis, as Winnemucca illustrates by including throughout the chapter the experiences of her older sister. That beautiful young woman is consistently threatened with assault and rape by various white settlers and officers, leading to her extreme but entirely justi-fied assertion that she "hate[s] everything that belongs to the white dogs" (38).

Yet Winnemucca also includes and responds to another tragedy in the passage immediately following the burial narrative, this one befalling a group of white settlers, and in so doing makes clear that fear and stasis are themselves perhaps the greatest and certainly the most avoidable threats facing these distinct but interconnected cul-tures. The section begins with an explicitly hostile cultural encoun-ter, the "fearful sight" of "the people that my grandfather called our white brothers" setting the tribe's winter supplies on fire for no apparent reason other than abject cruelty or fear. The fear at least is certainly mutual, as Winnemucca's people report that the settlers have "something like awful thunder and lightning, and with that they kill everything that [comes] in their way." Yet in the next lines Winnemucca steps back from those immediate and divisive cultural relationships to frame a larger and very distinct context: "This whole band of white people perished in the mountains, for it was too late to cross them. We could have saved them, only my people were afraid of them. We never knew who they were, or where they came from. So, poor things, they must have suffered fearfully, for they all starved there. The snow was too deep" (12–13).[5] The number of shifts contained in these few sentences is striking, starting with the reframing of the white settlers as "poor things" who "suffer fearfully" before meeting their fate. But more relevant to Winnemucca's point here is the sense that it is a combination of fear and ignorance (about a people's identity and origins) that leads to such a tragedy, and that if those negative elements of cultural perspective could be overcome, it would lead to more assured survival and salvation for the white settlers as well as the natives.

While that point might seem to be a very mature one, and thus part of Winnemucca's adult perspective in looking back on this early period in her life and cross-cultural experiences, she in fact highlights throughout the chapter her grandfather's attempts to convince not only the tribe overall but also and especially Winnemucca herself about the necessity for and benefits of such connections. After her first terrified glimpse of whites Winnemucca "imagine[s] I could see their big white eyes all night long," but her grandfather takes her aside and says "everything that was good about white people to" her; he supplements the lesson by showing her his "bright hat" and telling her about his experiences with Fremont during the Mexican War (25–26). Because of how important her grandfather's voice and perspective are to the young Winnemucca, partly as the tribal chief but especially as her most beloved family member, she takes his lesson very much to heart, noting that she "kept thinking over what he said to me about the good white people, and saying to myself, 'I will make friends with them when we come into California'" (27). When the traveling party reaches that destination, Winnemucca has a chance to experience for herself the potential for and benefits of such friendship, in response once again to unfamiliar and seemingly dangerous new contacts: she becomes extremely ill by contact with poison oak, her eyes swelling so painfully that it seems she might go blind; but is "made well," as her grandfather joyfully tells her, by the efforts of a "good white woman," his "white sister," who "put[s] some medicine on my face" and makes her see again. This time Winnemucca can supplement her grandfather's perspective with her own vision, literally and metaphorically: he claims that the woman is "truly an angel," and when the woman next visits, Winnemucca requests that her mother "fix my eyes so I can see the angel" and is rewarded with a view of, "indeed, a beautiful angel." That the woman herself has apparently lost a daughter, and that the clothes she gives Winnemucca are "her dead child's clothes," only adds to the sense that the connection made in this moment is literally familial, and that when Winnemucca concludes the section by noting, "So I came to love the white people," she is fulfilling her grandfather's vision and ideals very fully (31–33).

Although her opening chapter, after this shift, will continue to depict negative cultural encounters such as those experienced by her sister, it is on precisely these kinds of familial cross-cultural connections that Winnemucca focuses in the chapter's concluding pages. She reiterates those connections in her narration, stepping back to clarify for her "dear reader" that "there is no word so endearing as the word father, and that is why we call all good people, father or mother; no matter who it is,—negro, white man, or Indian, and the same with the women" (39). And she ends the chapter by ceding the narration one final time to her grandfather, as he delivers another extended oration to his tribe on the need to resist dwelling on the negative encounters and instead cement their insipient positive relationship with his "white brothers." He cites the practical arguments in favor of that step, noting that "they are already here in our land" and "we cannot tell them to go away." But he goes further, defining both cultures once more as part of a shared human family: "I know you won't say *kill them*. Surely you all know that they are human. Their lives as just as dear to them as ours to us." Winnemucca follows the oration with a final and telling cross-cultural analogy of the moment, noting that during the speech "now and then one could hear some of them cry out, just as the Methodists cry out at their meetings; and grandpa said a great many beautiful things to his people" (42–43). While the remainder of the narrative will move much more fully into Winnemucca's own voice and experiences, many of which further the darker encounters and images that this chapter has unquestionably foreshadowed, both it and her identity will develop with her grandfather's beautiful ideas and perspective as a clear and consistent foundation.

Her grandfather's influence is briefly but nicely illustrated by the next chapter, titled "Domestic and Social Moralities." The chapter's explicit goal is to serve as an ethnographic introduction to the Paiute people for an audience who, it is assumed, will be culturally distinct and thus largely or entirely unfamiliar with that community. Many of the chapter's specifics back up that purpose, from its consistent reliance on the first-person plural pronouns to one of its only explicit inclusions of the narrator's individual voice and identity, when Winnemucca uses herself to exemplify a tribal tradition: "I will repeat what we say of ourselves [at the flower-name dance]. 'I, Sarah Winnemucca, am a shell-flower, such as I wear on my dress. My name is Thocmetony'" (47). Even when Winnemucca begins to engage more overtly with political issues in the chapter, she does so through a similarly communal voice, one defined by the kinds of cultural divisions and fears introduced in chapter 1: "My people have been so unhappy for a long time they now wish to *disincrease,* instead of multiply. The mothers are afraid to have more children, for fear they shall have daughters, who are not safe even in their mother's presence" (48). In both its insider's ethnographic perspective and purpose and its broader cultural frame, then, the chapter seems to reiterate images of the native and white cultures as wholly distinct and, at least in their present circumstances, tragically opposed.

Yet the chapter's final pages complicate and undermine such images of cultural division and opposition in subtle but significant ways. For one thing, Winnemucca attributes the violence and wars between Native Americans and white settlers not to any innate cultural distinctions or divisions, but rather to a lack of knowledge of the fundamental similarities between the cultures: "But the whites have not waited to find out how good the Indians were, and what ideas they had of God, just like those of Jesus, who called him Father, just as my people do, and told men to do to others as they would be done by, just as my people teach their children to do" (51). Not only does Winnemucca highlight how closely the two cultures' spiritual and moral perspectives overlap—as she does later with their political systems, noting, "We have a republic as well as you" (53)—but she implicitly argues for the value of an interpreting ethnographic voice such as hers, one that can relate the unique aspects of her originating culture but also those cross-cultural interconnections between the cultures. The chapter likewise includes another cross-cultural voice making an impassioned case for such communication: in the text's longest editorial footnote, Mary Mann cites "one of [Winnemucca's] lectures" to argue for how much each culture would gain if "something like a human communication is established between the Indians and whites. It may prove a fair exchange," she notes, with the natives' "knowledge . . . enrich[ing] our early education as much as reading and writing will enrich theirs." While she cannot elide the divided perspectives and violent histories to which Winnemucca has alluded—Mann cites her fellow reformer Helen Hunt Jackson's *A Century of Dishonor* (1881) as thorough documentation for how "from the beginning the Christian bigots who peopled America looked upon the Indians as heathen"—she concludes with the earnest hope that "it is never too late to mend" (51–52). And it is precisely a cross-cultural voice and perspective like Winnemucca's that can establish such communication and produce such a future.

The awkward transition with which Winnemucca begins her subsequent chapter seems to indicate that her text will focus more on the divided and violent history than on the possibilities for cross-cultural communication. "I will now stop writing about myself and family and tribe customs, and tell about the wars, and the causes of the wars. I will jump over about six years," she opens chapter 3 (58). Certainly the subjects of her remaining chapters will, as their titles illustrate, be tied to the Paiute's communal experiences, and especially to some of their most opposed and hostile interactions with white settlers and American government: these include not only the "Wars and Their Causes" (chapter 3), such as "The Bannock War" (chapter 7), but also the tribe's multiple removals to reservations (chapters 5 and 8) and its abuse at the hands of Indian agents (chapter 6). Yet throughout these chapters, Winnemucca continues to construct her individual experiences and perspective, and behind them her evolving and hybrid identity and communities as an interpreter and mediator, as cross-cultural alternatives to those most negative relationships and encounters. It is thus far from coincidental that she depicts in the remainder of chapter 3's opening paragraph an ideal cross-cultural community in the town of Genoa (the first permanent white settlement in Nevada), one in which she and her sister "learn the English language very fast, for [their white host family] were very kind to us," and in which "all these white people [who were their neighbors] were loved by my people; we lived there together, and were as happy as could be" (58–59). If the wars and removals and abuses are Winnemucca's central and unavoidable historical subject, Genoa is the embodiment of her grandfather's cross-cultural vision and a foreshadowing of the community for which she will continually work during those years, and argue for throughout her narrative.

Significantly, Winnemucca contextualizes the events leading up to the first war between the region's Native Americans and white settlers with two implicit rejections of her grandfather's perspective and ideals. The first is the moment when, having learned of the murder of two white settlers by (they believe based on falsified evidence) Washoe natives, Winnemucca's kindly host Major Ormsbey and his men "sing the Star-spangled Banner. It was not a bit like the way my grandfather used to sing it," Winnemucca notes, "and that was the first time I had heard it sung by the white people" (60). Whereas the anthem had represented for her grandfather an occasion to demonstrate his familial embrace of American culture and identity, here it illustrates the moment when Winnemucca's ties to the Major and his community reach their cultural limits. The resulting cultural division is revealed shortly thereafter, when the Washoes bring in the three men whom they are sacrificing to appease the angry whites and the prisoners are met with hostility and violence. "Some said, 'Hang the red devils right off,' and the white boys threw stones at them, and used most shameful language to them" (61). While the stoning might seem to be the moment's most negative aspect, Winnemucca's structure highlights instead the shifts in perspective and language, the ways in which the white community— including its youngest and most impressionable voices—here define the natives entirely through the kinds of stereotypical images that are only possible in the absence of the communication and knowledge for which Winnemucca and Mann have argued. Winnemucca highlights in the chapter's concluding pages how much such division and hostility can negatively impact the native communities' own perspectives, limiting their futures well beyond the incident's specific ramifications: the Washoe chief laments of his lost men that "their blood is on my hands" and "their spirits will haunt me, and give me bad luck while I live" (63).

Winnemucca's grandfather's death, on which the brief chapter 4 ("Captain Truckee's Death") centers, seems to symbolize the loss of his cross-cultural dreams in this era of increasing cultural division and violence. "My grandfather was very sick at that time," Winnemucca writes in the chapter's opening sentence, and while the phrase refers literally to a coincidence in timing, it is easy to imagine that her grandfather is deeply troubled at the turn relations have taken with his white brothers (66). Similarly, the death of the family's "dear friend" Major Ormsbey, with the narration of which Winnemucca concludes her account of this first war, could also illustrate the breakdown of familial bonds between the cultures (72). Yet notwithstanding such tragic losses, the chapter as a whole depicts instead the continuing power and influence of her grandfather's perspective and vision. Providing that depiction first and foremost is her grandfather himself, who on his deathbed sends for "a dear beloved white brother of his" named Snyder, tells the man that he has "always love[d] you as if you were my dear son," and elicits from Snyder a promise to send Winnemucca and her siblings "to school to 'the sisters' at San José" (67). Winnemucca has highlighted throughout and reiterates here a great deal of evidence for her assertion that her grandfather was "great in principle" (69), and his ability to imagine and articulate these familial cross-cultural relationships is paramount on that list. That ability is also central to her grandfather's legacy, as illustrated by Winnemucca's brother's "brave deed" from later in the war: three neighbors, "Judge Broomfield and servant and a Spaniard," are threatened by native attackers despite the fact that they are "not fighting against" the tribe, and her brother "defend[s] their lives and risk[s] his own." As Winnemucca sadly notes, such cross-cultural actions "don't always get rewarded in this world," and her brother is "whipped . . . with a horsewhip" by his uncle "for saving white men's lives." But in alluding to another white friend, Mr. Seth Cook, whom her brother later saved and who "is still living, and can tell the story of his escape from death himself," Winnemucca makes clear that actions such as these ramify into the present and future just as powerfully as divisive and violent ones (72–73). If her brother extends their grandfather's legacy in those actions, it is Winnemucca who most fully extends it in her identity and role. The final, small but telling detail with which she concludes chapter 4 foreshadows both that inheritance and the particular talent with which Winnemucca will utilize it: "I have a dress which has been in our family a great many years. . . . I am going to wear it some time when I lecture." Winnemucca adds that the item is called "the mourning dress" (75), and that detail too is telling, since much of what she will document about her family's and culture's experiences will be tragic in the extreme. But while those tragedies are without question both specific to Native Americans and caused by white hostility and violence, they are also, Winnemucca makes clear throughout, the result of the worst kind of cross-cultural relationships and perspectives from all sides. Emblematic of those negative relationships are the figures on each side who, despite occupying roles that should allow them to facilitate cross-cultural understanding and connection, work instead to divide and harm the different communities for individual profit. Certainly that description applies to "the agents in [the Pyramid and Muddy Lake Reservation] agency" on whose "doings" Winnemucca dwells at length in chapter 5 (79); as she argues, these governmental mediators, far from protecting Native American interests or even attempting to keep the peace between the tribes and white settlers, consistently abuse native rights in order to "get rich very soon, so that they can have their gold-headed canes, with their names engraved on them" (86). But just as counterproductive and destructive are the voices of those "Indian interpreters who . . . easily get corrupted, and can be hired by the agents to do or say anything" (91); Winnemucca models that corrupt native voice in "Captain Dave," a man who can "always be hired to do a wicked thing," including "expos[ing] his wife to bad white men for money." That Dave is, she sadly admits, her "own cousin" only highlights how difficult it is for any member of these communities to extricate herself from the presence and influence of such negative voices (98).

Winnemucca likewise highlights in these chapters how family connections and tragic past experiences can contribute to negative cross-cultural encounters even for those community members who are not corrupt or driven by self-interest. She narrates for example the tragic death of her uncle "Truckee John," who is "killed by a man named Flamens, who claimed to have had a brother killed in the war of 1860. . . . Of course that had nothing to do with my uncle" (78), Winnemucca notes, suggesting how easily cross-cultural violence can become a cycle, producing future perspectives and actions that are defined entirely by past hostilities. Even the direct inheritor of her grandfather's role and legacy, Winnemucca's father, is not immune to that cycle: it is Winnemucca and her brother's sincere wish that their father "could only forget the wrong that the white men did to him," but they recognize that "of course he cannot forget it" (102), and those personal and cultural memories, while certainly more accurate than the ones that produced Flamens' murderous action, just as clearly limit her father's ability to imagine and contribute to more productive cross-cultural relationships and communities.

One way in which Winnemucca's narrative creates the opportunity for those more positive communities is, ironically, through her ability and willingness to narrate these violent and tragic histories. She writes of one such incident, the massacre of Paiute "old men, women and children" by US soldiers, that "it is a fearful thing to tell, but it must be told. Yes, it must be told by me" (77); while the telling of such brutalities could produce further cultural division and hostility, Winnemucca's explicit address in the same paragraph to her oft-included "dear reader" makes clear that she has a very different audience response in mind. Sympathetic horror is certainly part of that response, but even more productive for a genuinely communal future is her hope that white readers will contribute their own honest voices and cross-cultural experiences to the mix. Writing in the narrative's opening chapter about the help and sustenance that her people gave to the first settlers to arrive in the region, Winnemucca notes that "the persons I am speaking of are living yet; they could speak for us if they choose to do so" (10); her use of the conditional present tense is crucial to the sense—there and throughout the narrative—that she narrates the past precisely so as to influence the present and future. She is able to provide such a narration in large part due to a vital component of her own cross-cultural identity: her fluency in English. She writes in chapter 5 not only of corrupt and self-serving native interpreters but also of those who "are very ignorant, and don't understand English enough to know all that is said. This often makes trouble" (91) that is just as destructive as the explicitly hostile actions, and so her linguistic knowledge, and thus her ability to contribute to greater cross-cultural communication and understanding, is all the more needed and valuable. After all, she claims in delineating why she prefers to deal with the army rather than settlers or agents, "they know more about the Indians than any citizens do," and "nobody really knows Indians who cheat them and treat them badly" (93).

While her narrative can and does provide one vehicle through which Winnemucca can create such cross-cultural knowledge and communication, her identity as an interpreter constitutes another and even more active such means. That is particularly true when she helps avert cultural violence, as she does on multiple occasions in chapter 5 alone, for example saving an agent named Newgent by alerting him to an imminent attack and convincing him to "go away, quick!" (80); and, when her tribe's "warriors assemble, determined to begin a war to the death" in order to avenge a brutal murder, "talk[ing] and reason[ing] for hours, and at least persuad[ing] them to go to their camps" (104). But even the more mundane interpreter's work allows Winnemucca to create cross-cultural conversation in both directions where otherwise there would be no such opportunities. When a military officer writes to the tribe in regard to a recent hostile exchange, for example, her "people gather round me waiting for me to tell them something" about "what the paper said," and then explicitly argue that her ability to "speak to them on paper" mean that she is "the means of saving" them from a violent reprisal (82). Winnemucca likewise depicts her narrative itself as an act of interpretation to the "dear good Christian people" who are her ideal audience, an articulation of how her people, "who are called blood-seeking savages, are keeping our promises to the government" and are more than willing to engage in cross-cultural conversation with "those they respect and believe in" (89–90). Positioned as she is between these two communities and able to communicate the perspectives of each, it is Winnemucca's voice, both within the past being narrated and in that narrative's pages, that can best alter the stereotypical images, avert violence, and speak for the respectful and familial community that her grandfather had envisioned.

An interpreter's voice and role are cross-cultural and communal not only in their ability to speak in both directions but also, and with more complexity still, in their dependence on finding other, similarly ideal voices to interpret. Winnemucca both encounters such an ideal voice and experiences the difficulties of interpreting without one in the course of chapter 6, describing the Paiutes' time at "The Malheur Agency." The first agent for whom Winnemucca interprets there, Mr. Parrish, is by far the most positive and cross-cultural white voice she meets in the narrative, as she illustrates immediately by including a page-long oration of his to the tribe (her longest quote of a white voice). Parrish begins the speech by making an explicit familial connection with the tribe, noting that "now you are my children"; argues that, since in the future "the government is not always going to help us," it is vital for the tribe to work the land and sustain itself, not least because "the reservation is all" theirs; and promises that he "will build a school-house" and his "brother's wife will teach your children how to read like the white children," so that they can truly believe that "this is the best place for you all" in both the present and the future. While Parrish's perspective here could be described as paternalistic, the same word would apply to Winnemucca's grandfather, and like him Parrish both claims and demonstrates that he has "come here to do you good" (106–7). Moreover, he is entirely willing to hear and engage with Paiute perspectives, whether those that agree with his plan (such as subchief Egan) or those who prefer to continue hunting (such as subchief Oytes); and he learns of those perspectives because of how much he hears and values Winnemucca's voice. It is both to demonstrate his respect and to reiterate his goals for the tribe that Parrish smokes with the chiefs, admitting that "all my people say that [natives] won't work; but I will show them that you can work as well as anybody," and "will do all I can while I am with you." And his efforts convince even Winnemucca's bitter father, who asks "his people, ... don't you think this is the best father we ever had in all our lives?" (109).

Winnemucca's relationship with Parrish yields two of the text's most overt and successful cross-cultural collaborations. When Oytes attempts to convince Winnemucca that they are "two black ones" who "have not white fathers' lips," and thus to condone his decision to kill Parrish, she rejects the limiting cultural identity and helps avert the violence by instead warning the agent; Parrish for his part then diffuses Oytes' anger through dialogue and empathy, and the two men shake "hands, and [are] good friends afterwards" (114–15). Even more significant, if shorter-lived, is the triumphant completion of the promised schoolhouse, an effort to which Winnemucca contributes on multiple levels: convincing Parrish to hire her blind cousin Jarry as his new interpreter, so she can take a job alongside Mrs. Parrish "teaching the children English"; participating in the joyous opening ceremony in which she leads the native children in singing "as well as they could" for both her people and visiting whites; and working diligently with the over four hundred young pupils to assure that they "learn very fast, and [are] glad to come to school" (116). While Winnemucca's individual fluency in English is enough to facilitate her cross-cultural interpreting, such a school is necessary if the community as a whole is to move closer to her identity and her grandfather's dream. And when Winnemucca notes, in a rare confession of speechlessness, that she "cannot tell or express how happy we were" at the school's success, it is perhaps because in this endeavor her people can speak for themselves (116–17).

Unfortunately the school, like Parrish's efforts as agent overall, seems to be too cross-cultural, not sufficiently orthodox in culture, for the federal authorities, and Parrish receives word that he is to be replaced; he is, the letter "from your Big Father in Washington" notes, "not a Christian, and all the reservations [are] to be under the Christian men's care" (117–18). The new agent, Reinhard, immediately reverses Parrish's cross-cultural gestures and perspective: telling the tribe that "this land which you are living on is government land" and that the "government will give you work" if they obey its directives; and making clear that his role and voice will be similarly hierarchical and monologic: "When I tell you to do anything I don't want any of you to dictate to me, but to go and do it" (124–25). If Parrish's presence allowed Winnemucca to maximize her interpreter's role and begin extending her identity to the tribe as a whole, this kind of negative cross-cultural voice reveals instead the limitations inherent in that role and identity. As Winnemucca admits to Reinhard, as his interpreter "whatever you say to me I am always ready to do my duty as far as it goes" (128), and that dependence creates a division between Winnemucca and her tribe and family throughout this section. That division is caused initially by her inability to converse with Reinhard as an equal and help plan the tribe's future: Egan and others ask Winnemucca if they are to "lose our home" and be removed to another reservation, and she can only reply that she has "nothing to say. I am only here to talk for you all" (126). But when Reinhard uses Winnemucca's interpreting voice to threaten a young Paiute boy, the division becomes more overt, with her cousin Jarry noting that it does not seem "right" for her to collaborate with the agent in such a situation; Winnemucca can only respond that she has "not told anything but what I was told to tell them," and the reply seems unsatisfying both for her communal role and her individual identity (128).

Yet Winnemucca does not end the conversation, much less her narrative, with that sentiment. When Jarry seems to lose hope for the tribe's future in the face of Reinhard's threats, she replies, "Dear brother, I am ashamed of you, you talk so heartlessly. I am going to see my people dealt rightly by, and to stand by them, and I am going to talk for them just as long as I live" (129). The "dear brother" echoes the "dear reader" address that Winnemucca uses throughout the narrative, and Winnemucca focuses here entirely on the power of language and voice: the danger of heartless talk on the one hand; and her ability to talk for her people, implicitly but crucially to the white community, on the other. Although she continues to recognize and respond to the limits of an interpreting voice, quitting her job as Reinhard's interpreter and even stealing a letter of his to ascertain his plans for the tribe, she is both unable and unwilling to abandon her role as a mediating figure between these communities: the next chapter begins with tribal representatives asking her, since she is "the only one that is always ready to talk for" them, to "write on paper to our good father in Washington" (140). Even when the situation turns into "The Bannock War" of the chapter's title and Winnemucca attempts to cede authority to the tribe's male warriors, they respond that she "know[s] what to do" and that "whatever you say we will follow" her (156). Yet at the same time that it uniquely positions her to help and guide the Paiutes, Winnemucca's cross-cultural identity continues to divide her from that culture in this chapter, as evidenced when Egan concludes a long speech to a white military officer by noting that they "are at a loss to know which of you are right: whether Sam Parrish told us lies or you, or our chieftain's daughter, Sarah Winnemucca, about the land being ours" (146).

Indeed, this chapter, the narrative's longest, depicts throughout the multipart communal and individual effects of Winnemucca's evolving cross-cultural role and identity. For one thing, while Winnemucca's efforts once again help end a war and "save my father and his people," the situation in this case is significantly more complex than in the earlier ones: the opposing sides are both comprised of Paiutes, with Oytes leading the forces threatening Winnemucca's father; as a result, Winnemucca leads a diplomatic expedition that includes not only Paiutes but also a number of US military officers (all of whose names and ranks she lists, as if to emphasize how many important whites were under her command). Moreover, whereas she has framed prior peacemaking efforts as explicitly undertaken "for her people," in this case she defines them as much more specific to her individual, cross-cultural identity: "This was the hardest work I ever did for the government in all my life. . . . Yes, I went for the government when the officers could not get an Indian man or a white man to go for love or money." The general (Howard) in charge of the US forces confirms this new leadership role, asking Winnemucca to serve as his "interpreter and guide" throughout and after the conflict (164–65). While the role seems both surprising and difficult to comprehend for many of the whites—when a group of soldiers see Winnemucca among the officers they "cry out, 'Oh, . . . they have Sarah Winnemucca a prisoner'" (165) and later a white settler who is "always ready to condemn" Winnemucca asks an officer why they are "tak[ing] so much trouble in taking her to Camp Harney" (168)—the support that Winnemucca receives from soldiers in parallel leadership roles confirms her status. Lieutenant Wilkinson rebuts the settler's perspective with a direct appeal to Winnemucca's individual identity, noting that the woman does not "know what [she is] talking about. This is Sarah Winnemucca" (168); and the general revises the cultural hierarchy as a result of his encounters with Winnemucca, telling her that her "people have good hearts, better than these white dogs have" (166).

Those shifts in cultural perspectives likewise reflect Winnemucca's own evolving ideas about and relationships to whites throughout this chapter. Just as Parrish had illustrated for Winnemucca that not all whites fall into the stereotypical category of "Christian" that she had come to associate with the most corrupt agents, so too she encounters here a group of sympathetic army officers with identities outside of that type, and presents them in her narrative as another interesting ethnographic detail: "White men, educated, not Christians; men that are almost born with the Bible in hand. What! not Christians? Yes, that is just what I mean" (165). She experiences a more personal and striking perspective shift about one white man, "a newspaper reporter of the name of Parker from Walla-Walla" (174). Parker initially accuses Winnemucca of being "the one that started [her] people on the war-path," but when she confronts him with the lie and reminds him that she had once fed him when he was starving, he repents and asks her to "forgive me"; she calls him a "brute" but apparently does so in good humor, as she notes that he "turned out afterwards to be the best friend I had" (166). More intimately still, she receives an offer of marriage from a white single father, Morton, with whom she has traveled for a time: Morton's daughter Rosey "has come to love" Winnemucca, and Morton, in an effort to keep the unconventional but blossoming family intact, asks Winnemucca to "go to Silver City and get married right away." Although Winnemucca turns him down, she perceives the "kind offer" as an "honor," and couches her refusal as entirely unrelated to cultural differences or identities, but rather because she "cannot marry a man that I don't love" (151).[6]

Rosey and her father emblematize not only Winnemucca's expanding cross-cultural community but also the many ways in which she begins to create a family of her own in this chapter, extending her existing tribal family to the multiple communities with which she now associates. She becomes a sort of mother figure to young white soldiers, particularly those who have been wounded in battle: she notes how much her "heart used to ache for the poor soldiers" (185), and recounts at length a night she spends with a dying soldier, answering his plea for "some one to come to him" in his final moments (178). She likewise takes on a fuller motherly role to the tribe than at any prior point, as evidenced by the moment when she interprets the general's instructions to a tribal representative but adds her own addendum: "Tell them I, their mother, say come back to their homes again. I will stand by them and see that they are not sent away to the Indian Territory" (182). She even becomes a more literal mother for a time, to "a little girl-baby" whom the army discovers after a battle and for whom Winnemucca cares for three months: the soldiers soon come to call the baby Winnemucca's own, and even when the child's mother and father are found and the actual family reunited, Winnemucca notes that "all [her] people and the officers called this little baby my baby, and they named it Sarah" (199–200). It is, I would argue, precisely because she has taken on these cross-cultural leadership roles on so many levels—military, diplomatic, familial—that Winnemucca can return to her original community at chapter's end as a new and more powerful leader there as well: her father tells the assembled tribe that his "child's name is so far beyond yours. . . . Her name is everywhere and every one praises her . . . [she] has saved so many lives, not only mine, but a great many, both whites and her own people. Now hereafter we will look on her as our chieftain, for none of us are worthy of being chief but her" (193). It is in this moment, more than any other, that Winnemucca assumes the legacy of her grandfather's role and ideals, both for the tribe and in his hoped-for, cross-cultural, national family.

The narrative's concluding chapter presents a particularly difficult situation for the tribe and its new chief, as they are forced, despite Winnemucca's earlier promise about Indian Territory, to relocate to a reservation at Yakima. Because of how directly the move contradicts Winnemucca's prior statements, she acknowledges that it might exacerbate the worst elements of her interpreter's role and thoroughly divide her from the tribe, exclaiming that her "people will never believe me again" (204). The major who tells Winnemucca the bad news inadvertently highlights that division, attempting to reassure her initial worries by noting that the news is "nothing about you; it is about your people" (203). But if the situation does exemplify some of the most negative aspects of Winnemucca's new role and identity, it also allows her to express, in two of her narrative's most significant and eloquent passages, meaningful critiques of and hopes for the expanding America of which she is now so much a part. In the first, briefer passage, Winnemucca responds to the relocation order, which is to be executed in the harshest winter conditions, by asking the officer "what can the President be thinking about? . . . Is he man or beast? Yes, he must be a beast; if he has no feeling for my people. . . . I have never seen a president in my life and I want to know whether he is made of wood or rock, for I cannot for once think that he can be a human being" (205). And when the day for the forced march arrives, Winnemucca builds upon but also creates an alternative to those national critiques, in her longest direct address to an American audience:

> Oh, for shame! You who are educated by a Christian government in the art of war; the practice of whose profession makes you natural enemies of the savages, so called by you. Yes, you, who call yourselves the great civilization; you who have knelt upon Plymouth Rock, covenanting with God to make this land the home of the free and the brave. Ah, then you rise from your bended knees and seizing the welcoming hands of those who are the owners of this land, which you are not, your carbines rise from the bleak shore, and your so-called civilization sweeps inland from the ocean wave; but, oh, my God! leaving its pathway marked by crimson lines of blood, and strewed by the bones of two races, the inheritor and the invader; and I am crying out to you for justice—yes, pleading for the far-off plains of the West, for the dusky mourner, whose tears of love are pleading for her husband, or their children, who are sent far away from them. (207)

Winnemucca's profoundly powerful oration here does not minimize the brutal, violent, and divided history that has comprised so many native and white encounters in the centuries after contact; but she consciously frames that history in the context of the idealized American history of Plymouth and covenant, and in so doing creates the possibility of a different future, one in which welcome and community take the place of weapon and war, and in which the voices of Native Americans and the West are added to an expanded national anthem.

Winnemucca also stresses throughout her concluding chapter and materials how much her own, cross-cultural voice is ideally suited to make those expansive arguments. She does so in part by arguing against the "civilized and Christian" Native Americans who are often privileged by the agents and authorities over other natives (211); Winnemucca links these civilized natives to hypocritical Christian agents who "steal and tell lies" (214), but even more tellingly critiques their inability to learn and speak English. "Of course one who did not know them might think they were educated when they heard them sing English songs," she admits, "but I assure you they did not know what they sang any more than I know about logarithms" (216); her use of the complex mathematical term nicely reminds the reader of how strong her own grasp of the language is in comparison to these only superficially cross-cultural natives. She likewise highlights here the opportunities and successes that her strong voice and cross-cultural identity provide: she travels to San Francisco and Washington, DC, to deliver lectures that make, as Mann adds in a footnote, a "very great impression" (217); when she meets with resistance in the latter city from an employee of the Secretary of the Interior, she is asked by a new white friend to deliver an impromptu and unscheduled lecture, since "this is a free country" and "they can't stop" her (222); and she even takes advantage of a surprise meeting with President Hayes and his wife in Vancouver to deliver her message directly, telling him, in the narrative's penultimate paragraph, "You are a husband and father, and you know how you would suffer to be separated from your wife and children by force, as my people still are, husbands from wives, parents from children." She notes with pride that "Mrs. Hayes cried all the time I was talking, and he said, 'I will see about it,'" this most powerful audience convinced by Winnemucca's eloquence and strength (246).

The narrative's closing sentence highlights how much Winnemucca's role and identity remain and will always be closely tied to her Paiute culture and community. "After my marriage to Mr. Hopkins," she writes, "I visited my people once more at Pyramid Lake Reservation, and they urged me again to come to the East and talk for them, and so I have come" (246). The abrupt and striking shift to the present tense in the final clause makes clear how much Winnemucca's people and past are with her as she figuratively stands before her eastern white audience and concludes the extended act of interpreting that community's wrongs and claims that has constituted much of her narrative. Yet she follows this final line with an appendix, and includes there not only a series of letters and documents from white officers and officials in support of her narrative and voice but also one final statement of her own, an argument for her individual identity and role. "Those who have maligned me have not known me," she claims, for when she is able to communicate her experiences and identity, it is clear that she has "been sincere with my own people when they have done wrong, as well as with my white brothers." The cross-cultural, familial equity and fairness of that sentiment reminds Winnemucca one final time of her "dear old grandfather" and his vision of unity with "his white brothers, whom he loved so much." Her grandfather did not live to see that cross-cultural community achieved, and Winnemucca admits that as of this moment her people's "white brothers have given them neither love nor truth" (258). Yet her role and voice have allowed Winnemucca, like her contemporaries Lewis Henry Morgan and Ely Parker, to bridge the gap, to provide both of those vital elements to both of these cultural communities, and in so doing to imagine an expanded future America that can fulfill her grandfather's prophesied tradition and meet her ideal interpretations.

5

Transformative Mixtures

Gloria Anzaldúa's Hybrid Mosaic

"No Name Woman," the opening section of Maxine Hong Kingston's *The Woman Warrior: Memoirs of a Girlhood Among Ghosts* (1976), makes a compelling case for the personal and cultural investigations and understandings that are at the core of ethnic studies and multiculturalism. While both the section and the book are, as their titles suggest, deeply concerned with issues of gender and sexuality, Kingston grounds those issues in even more fundamental questions about ethnic heritage and identity as they influenced her early life as the daughter of Chinese immigrants to America. Having begun the section with her mother's voice narrating a particularly harrowing family story from China (a village's brutal killing of her unmarried and pregnant aunt), Kingston steps back to raise those questions with an audience in the exact same ethnic category and situation as herself: "Chinese-Americans, when you try to understand what things in you are Chinese, how do you separate what is peculiar to childhood [and various other specific realities] . . . from what is Chinese?" (5–6). She likewise connects her interest in her aunt's story and her family's Chinese history to her attempts to define her identity in the present, noting that "unless I see her life branching into mine, she gives me no ancestral help" (8). In acknowledging and engaging with her aunt's story, Kingston explicitly rebels against her mother's traditional Chinese perspective, her orders that Kingston not "tell anyone you had an aunt," because her "father does not want to hear her name" (15); but she also frames the story as an alternative to a mainstream American identity, to her previous attempts to "turn myself American-feminine, . . . make myself American-pretty" (11–12). So it is perhaps most accurate to say that, by "devot[ing] pages of paper to" her aunt (16) and all the others whose stories she tells in the book, Kingston attempts to answer her own foundational question, to determine what in her—not her family's or her culture's, but her individual—Chinese-American identity is Chinese, and what those ethnic ghosts mean for her present self and life.

Kingston's second book, *China Men* (1980), comprises in some ways a direct continuation of that storytelling and those investigations and analyses, connected in this case to the male members of Kingston's extended family and, through them, additional aspects of her Chinese culture and heritage. But Kingston's purpose in *China Men* lies less in identifying and narrating what is Chinese in her identity and more in portraying and analyzing the complex, cross-cultural experiences and identities at the heart of her family's Chinese-American story. That difference is immediately apparent through the book's section titles, which reference those cross-cultural experiences in multiple ways: the book opens with a section titled "The Father from China," but then moves to "The Great Grandfather of the Sandalwood Mountains" (a range in Hawaii) and "The Great Grandfather of the Sierra Nevada Mountains," making clear that her family's geographic and cultural trajectory has been multidirectional and multinational for many generations; Kingston follows those two sections with "The Making of More Americans," after which, as if to prove how cultural identities cannot remain static or stable in the face of such constant movement and change, she reenvisions her father as "The American Father." At the outset Kingston asks of her father the same kinds of cultural questions with which she began the first book, wondering if he "mean[s] to give us a chance at being real Americans by forgetting the Chinese past?" and admitting that, while he "fix[es himself] in the present," she "want[s] to hear the stories about the rest of [his] life, the Chinese stories" (14–15). But by the "American Father" section she has come to terms with the difficulty of separating out the different cultural stories that compose her father's Chinese-American life, admitting that "maybe his village was America" (237). And the

book opens and closes with brief, broader pieces that contextualize this cross-cultural emphasis: the opening, "On Discovery," creates a cross-cultural mythology, envisioning a "Women's Land" that
"some scholars say . . . was discovered" in seventh-century China
and "some say earlier than that, . . . and it was in North America" (5);
and the closing, "On Listening," emphasizes cross-culture history,
with "a Filipino scholar" narrating the mostly untold experiences
of Chinese-Filipino immigrants to an ethnically diverse group of
"young men who listen" (307–8). Every element of Kingston's work,
from the central personal and familial investigations to the mythological and historical contexts for those stories, is in *China Men*
grounded in cross-cultural experiences and identities.

   Much of American culture in the last few decades of the twentieth century was dominated by the rise of identity politics, ethnic
studies, and multiculturalism in its many forms, and a primary
goal of those movements was to help both individual Americans
and broader communities become more aware of and sensitive to
the connections between their own and others' identities and ethnic and racial heritages and communities (as well as communities
organized around gender, sexual preference, and many other factors). Just as is the case for Kingston in both books (especially *The
Woman Warrior*), learning about and communicating those identities and heritages is often profoundly productive and powerful, not
only for the individual and community in question, but also for all
those other Americans to whom the stories can be told. But as I
argue in my introduction, in one important way multiculturalism
and its concurrent movements can be as limiting as the traditional
narrative that has been their near-constant opponent in the culture
wars of the last few decades: both perspectives emphasize the presence and influence of relatively distinct and static cultures in American history and identity, with the difference really about numbers
(one founding culture versus many) and hierarchy ("other" cultures
becoming more like "ours" in the traditional melting pot narrative;
all cultures maintaining their own distinct flavor in the multicultural stew version). As the family experiences and broader contexts
through which Kingston frames *China Men* illustrate, the realities
for any individual American and for any American community are
significantly more intricate, and more defined by cross-cultural

shifts, than either of those alternatives allow. It is the seminal work of another prominent American author of the multicultural age, Gloria Anzaldúa, that best portrays, analyzes, and embodies those complex and cross-cultural realities. While Anzaldúa's *Borderlands/ La Frontera: The New Mestiza* (1987) is invested in describing a distinct, if relatively new and nuanced, cultural identity, that of Chicanos, she also and most importantly works throughout the text to create a new category, "mestiza," a mixed community that can include individuals from across cultures and can as a result capture and communicate America's cross-cultural history and identity. And Anzaldúa's book represents as well as narrates that mestiza community, creating in its forms and themes a hybrid mosaic that comprises the many components in an alternative, cross-cultural definition of America.[1]

On the surface, literally, Anzaldúa's book seems in one way to reflect the era of identity politics and multiculturalism: its publisher, Aunt Lute Books, categorizes it on its back cover as both women's studies and Chicano studies, two academic disciplines that emerged directly out of the social movements of the late 1960s and 1970s and would blossom with the scholarly and cultural trends of the 1980s. While Chicano studies is more specifically cultural than women's studies, both are equally connected to a particular, relatively static community and explicitly distinct from an outside community (non-Chicanos and men, respectively). The two terms that constitute the book's main title could be read as reinforcing the Chicano studies emphasis, both in their focus on the border (the Mexican-American border was in the 1980s undergoing one of its periodic, cyclical moments as a site of national controversy and supposed crisis) and in the use of both the English and Spanish terms for that region (as if to translate the English title into Spanish for a Chicano audience). Both of those elements are at once highlighted and complicated by the cover's graphic design—the title's two terms are separated not by the backslash with which I divide them but by a long, horizontal, thick yet wavy black line, one that partly reinforces the divisions inherent in a border (with the English term above the Spanish, which could be read as either geographic or hierarchical) and partly implies how porous such separations will prove in Anzaldúa's narrative. And the subtitle more explicitly introduces the latter possibility, combining English and Spanish into one hybrid phrase and concurrently foregrounding, in the word "mestiza," the concept of mixture through which Anzaldúa will challenge any and all static images of culture and identity. No doubt aware of the parallel challenge that her hybrid text will present to even the most sympathetic readers, Anzaldúa introduces the work with a brief preface that establishes her central ideas clearly and concisely (making a strong case for many of my own project's arguments and methodologies in the process). While her opening sentence acknowledges that there is an "actual physical borderland" that she is "dealing with in this book, the Texas-US Southwest/ Mexican border," she quickly moves away from that specific geographic and cultural definition of her subject and into the many other meanings she hopes to impart to the phrase. The most vital such meanings are explicitly cross-cultural: "The Borderlands are physically present," she writes, "wherever two or more cultures edge each other, where people of different races occupy the same territory." Lest this definition still seem to depend on distinct, static, and opposed cultures or races, she makes clear in the next paragraph that she will be concerned with the ways in which even individual identity—and thus certainly the communities composed of such individuals—is itself already cross-cultural: "I am a border woman. I grew up between two cultures . . . I have been straddling that *tejas*-Mexican border, and others, all my life." She admits the discomforts and pains that come with such cross-cultural experiences and identities, but makes a strong case for the "compensations" and "certain joys" that can be produced by "living on borders and in margins, keeping intact one's shifting and multiple identity and integrity." And while she opposes that cross-cultural state to vague images of mainstream "society's clamor to uphold the old, to rejoin the flock, to go with the herd," I would argue that her descriptions of this "landscape, . . . this place of contradictions," quite nicely capture the cross-cultural America that has existed in all its forms and iterations throughout the prior four centuries (19).

If Anzaldúa's preface thus lays out the cross-cultural national identity for which my project argues, it also compellingly locates that identity in personal narratives. On one level, Anzaldúa identifies cross-cultural identity as a primary—even primal—source for her text, linking her "almost instinctive urge to communicate, to speak, to write about life on the borders" to the "unique positioning consciousness takes at these confluent streams." But she goes further, arguing that "this book . . . speaks of my existence," explicitly connecting the text's identity to her own; she drives home the stakes inherent in that idea by noting that "books . . . taught me first how to survive and then how to soar" and that her "passion for the daily struggle to render [images and words] concrete in the world and on paper, to render them flesh, keeps me alive." To write a personal narrative, then, is to narrate and sustain one's life in the future as well as the past, to capture and recreate an identity in all its complexity and vitality. Anzaldúa likewise links a key aspect of the text's hybrid nature (and its difficulty), its multilingual "switching of 'codes,'" to her "language, a new language—the language of the Borderlands." She does identify that language (and thus implicitly herself) with a particular culture, naming it "Chicano Spanish," but undercuts any potential limits of that phrase by noting that "at the juncture of cultures, languages cross-pollinate and are revitalized." Similarly, she concludes the preface by highlighting how the individual identity represented in a personal narrative extends outwards to the communities of readers with which it engages: "This book is our invitation to you," she writes, "from the new *mestizas*." The sentence suggests a potential, limiting division between "us" and "you," implying what we could call the multicultural goals for Anzaldúa's book: adding "mestiza" to the list of founding American cultures; producing one more line on the census form. But the preface as a whole, and particularly its descriptions of a border identity that mirrors America's founding and ongoing cross-cultural experiences and is best captured by personal narratives of those experiences, foreshadows the many ways in which mestiza culture will be the central component of the individual and communal American identities that Anzaldúa's book defines and embodies (19–20).

Anzaldúa also provides, in two crucial and culminating passages from her book's two halves, metatextual extensions of these opening concepts. In the opening pages of the prose first half's penultimate (sixth) chapter, Anzaldúa steps back to consider, in a long and dense paragraph, "this book that I'm almost finished writing." She does so because "the work has an identity," and the phrase's final word is entirely apt; every line of her description also reflects both her own and the nation's cross-cultural identities. More exactly, there are three particularly salient sentences in which Anzaldúa describes her book. First, she notes that she "see[s] a mosaic pattern . . . emerging, a weaving pattern," and the image captures both the multiplicity of constituent elements and their intertwined, inseparable relationship. She then highlights the "hybridization of metaphor, different species of ideas popping up here, popping up there, full of variations and seeming contradictions"; this image acknowledges the diversity and difficulty that accompany a truly hybrid identity, but Anzaldúa subsequently extends the implication of "seeming contradictions" by reaffirming her "belie[f] in" that identity's ultimate unity, in "an ordered, structured universe where all phenomena are interrelated and imbued with spirit." In her third description, she depicts "this almost finished product [as] an assemblage, a montage, a beaded work with several leitmotifs and with a central core," paralleling the hybrid mosaic to those related artistic concepts, ones that do not elide the distinct individual components (a montage depends on their differences for its structure) but that provide additional symbols for their interconnected and communal core. And she concludes the paragraph by admitting that community's far from ideal nature ("it is a flawed thing—a clumsy, complex, groping blind thing") but also its ongoing and evolving promise ("for me it is alive, infused with spirit")—a promise, she makes clear in her brief final sentence ("I talk to it; it talks to me"), that depends on the dialogic presence and participation of every individual within the community (88–89).

Anzaldúa creates a similarly dialogic and evolving representation of cross-cultural identity in the poem "To live in the Borderlands means you," located in the poetic second half's sixth and final chapter. The poem's very title, which enjambs directly into the first stanza, immediately involves the audience in its constructions of a hybrid identity, one that the first stanza's complex, multilingual single sentence drives home: "are neither *hispana india negra española / ni gabacha, eres mestiza, mulata* half-breed / caught in the crossfire between camps / while carrying all five races on your back / not knowing which side to turn to, run from." Each subsequent stanza extends that initial image and further exemplifies the dangers, the benefits, and above all the meanings of such a border identity, one that time and again resists any static categorizations (cultural or otherwise): "denying the Anglo inside you / is as bad as having denied the Indian or Black"; "forerunner of a new race, / half and half—both woman and man, neither—/a new gender"; "put *chile* in the borscht, / . . . speak Tex-Mex with a Brooklyn accent." After seven such parallel stanzas, Anzaldúa shifts dramatically in the poem's final, briefest and most overt stanza: "To survive the Borderlands / you must live *sin fronteras* / be a crossroads." These closing lines move the poem's setting from past and present to a conditional future, one in which the poem's and book's title can be transcended if the hybrid individual identity takes on the communal and connective role of a crossroads: bringing different paths together and, if the borders are truly transcended, moving them forward onto a shared road.

As if to foreshadow that culminating poem, Anzaldúa opens the book's first prose chapter with a three-page poem depicting numerous such crossroads. The poem's first stanza presents a natural intersection, "the edge where earth touches ocean / where the two overlap," and in the second stanza that natural presence disrupts Anzaldúa's most foundational, geographic border: "silver waves marbled with spume / gashing a hole under the border fence." When Anzaldúa introduces herself as the poem's speaker, in the fifth stanza, she does so through both an action and a typographic choice that embraces such transgression: "I walk   through the hole in the fence / to the other side." The two-space gap between "walk" and "through," the text's first such typographical element, illustrates what a hole can accomplish—breaking the accepted tradition that the fence implies, forcing us to recognize how porous such borders always are and allowing us to follow Anzaldúa as she moves across the space between. In the next stanza, we see that she is far from the only such crosser: "Beneath the iron sky / Mexican children kick their soccer ball across, / run after it, entering the U.S." Neither the sea nor such inadvertent border crossings can entirely elide the fence's powerful and destructive presence, as Anzaldúa fully admits, describing the fence as a "1,950 mile-long open wound / dividing a *pueblo*, a culture, / running down the length of my body, / staking fence rods in my flesh, / splits me   splits me / *me raja   me raja.*"

Here the textual holes represent division rather than border cross-ing, but both Anzaldúa's repetition of the singular article "a" and her association of her body with that single unifying culture under-mines those divisions, pointing toward the image of a bridge with which the poem concludes. "*Yo soy un puente tendido / del mundo gabacho al del mojado,*" Anzaldúa writes in the final stanza, position-ing both herself and her text as that bridge that can span the gap and tie those worlds together. And in the subsequent, initial prose para-graph, she makes clear that all those who "live here" in the Border-lands, which exists "in a constant state of transition," can perform that role, designating these "inhabitants . . . *los atravesados:* . . . those who cross over, pass over, or go through" (23–25).

Anzaldúa uses a more specific bridge, the land bridge from Asia, to introduce the first component of a cross-cultural American identity as she will construct it: an alternative narrative of American history. In that historical narrative, the founding culture is not the Puritans, nor the Spanish explorers, nor even the Native American tribes whom both those European arrivals encountered, but instead can be traced back to "the original peopling of the Americas," when "the first inhabitants migrated across the Bering Straits and walked south across the continent." Anzaldúa references this "oldest evidence of humankind in the U.S." partly to connect Chicano culture to that originating moment—she calls this founding culture "the Chicanos' ancient Indian ancestors"—but mostly to argue that America has always been constituted by movement and shift, as illustrated by the verbs ("migrated" three times, "walked," "left," "guided") that drive these first historical paragraphs (26–27). She immediately connects those geographic crossings to more explicitly cultural ones, high-lighting the prominent role played from early in this alternative historical narrative by "the *mestizos*" in "found[ing] a new hybrid race, . . . a race that had never existed before." Moreover, even that hybrid product represents not an endpoint of the narrative but rather an illustration of its continual development, as "the continual intermarriage between Mexican and American Indians and Span-iards formed an even greater *mestizaje*" (27). And Anzaldúa links both the geographic and cross-cultural crossings into an affirma-tion of an alternative American community, one that certainly could claim Cabeza de Vaca as one of its foundational figures: "We have a tradition of migration, a tradition of long walks" (33).[2]

Much of the rest of this chapter's alternative American history would seem to undermine such attempts at constructing a unified, communal identity and tradition. Beginning with the paragraph immediately after the "intermarriage" sentence, Anzaldúa traces a history in which Anglos and Mexicans are in violent opposition: "In the 1800s, Anglos migrated illegally into Texas," she opens that paragraph, and the verb "migrated" here, coupled with the "illegally" so often applied to Mexican immigrants to the United States, takes on a distinctly more divisive and hostile connotation than in its prior appearances (28). Many of the history's remaining topics and descriptions reinforce that division: "the Battle of the Alamo, in which the Mexican forces vanquished the whites" (28); "in 1846, the U.S. incited Mexico to war" (29); "[in 1915], the Anglos, afraid that the *mexicanos* would seek independence from the U.S., brought in 20,000 army troops" (30); "North Americans call this [late-twentieth-century] return to the homeland the silent invasion" (32). In each of these moments Anzaldúa could be seen as simply revising an Anglo-centric narrative of American history to produce instead a Chicano-centric one, an act of rebalancing that, while politically and culturally understandable, would likely result in no more cross-cultural a history than the original one.

Yet there is another way to read her intent here, one more focused on revising the concept of an ethnocentric perspective and history and suggesting a replacement for the resulting gap in our national narratives. In another passage that would seem to portray and recreate cultural division, Anzaldúa writes that "the Gringo, locked into the fiction of white superiority, seized complete political power, stripping Indians and Mexicans of their land while their feet were still rooted in it" (29). But if white superiority is a fiction, so too, perhaps, is the idea of "the gringo" as separate from these other cultures; that sense of separation, after all, is necessary if one culture is to displace others from their shared land and roots. In describing the effect of this displacement, Anzaldúa notes that "we were jerked out by the roots, truncated, disemboweled, dispossessed, and separated from our identity and our history" (30), and this too can be read as the destruction not only of a particular culture or cultures but also and more significantly of the communal, cross-cultural American identity and history that the chapter's alternative narrative has delineated. It is through that lens, I would argue, that Anzaldúa later describes illegal immigrants from Mexico to the United States as "refugees in a homeland that does not want them" (34): according to the traditional, culturally divisive narrative and categories, these people are illegal and undesirable; but in Anzaldúa's alternative history, they are coming back to their home, returning to the roots and identity that they share with all the other individuals and cultures who have migrated to this cross-cultural place.

The title of the book's second chapter, "*Movimientos de rebeldía y las culturas que traicionan* [Movements of Rebellion and the Cultures that They Betray]," makes more explicit Anzaldúa's argument that her creation and embrace of an alternative, cross-cultural identity will require her to "betray" all the static cultures to which she might belong (rather than simply embrace a revisionist Chicano culture and perspective in opposition to Anglo ones). She initially presents that process of cultural rejection as profoundly individual: the chapter's long opening epigraph (in Spanish) notes that she is "filled with rage when someone—be it my mother, the Church, the Anglo culture—tells me do this, do that without considering my desires," and indicates her decision to "no longer spend my life dumping cultural customs and values that betrayed me" (37); and the opening pages expand upon that frame, narrating her need to "disengage from my family, my *tierra*, my *gente*," to "leave home so I could find myself" and be true to "my strong sense of who I was and what I was about." She uses a very telling fact—that she "was the first in six generations to leave the Valley, the only one in my family to ever leave home"—to drive home how individual and unique that choice was. And when she begins to theorize the underlying meaning of her departure, she does so first by portraying it as a choice to reject communal narratives (the "cultural tyranny" that values "tribal rights over those of the individual" and defines "the individual . . . first as kin . . . and last as self") and to embrace instead her most intimate self, the "rebel in me—the Shadow-Beast" that "hates constraints of any kind, even those self-imposed" (38–40). While every individual might well benefit from such an embrace, it is unclear in these initial pages how a new community could be constituted out of such choices and experiences.

The remainder of the chapter works to create precisely such a community, however, to imagine a communal identity comprised of such experiences and—even more importantly—positively influencing the other communities to which it connects. Anzaldúa explicitly defines that community here through gender and sexual orientation, noting the link between her identity and those of "other queer people" by highlighting the rebellions necessary to be a "lesbian of color" (41). But in writing that for such women their "face[s are] caught between *los intersticios,* the spaces between the different worlds we inhabit" (42), Anzaldúa links their identity and situation overtly to the mestiza community that she has begun to narrate; she similarly highlights this identity's potential mediating role in a broader community divided along (for example) cultural lines, its providing of "a way of balancing, of mitigating duality" (41). She represents each individual's cultural rebellion through the same deeply significant image with which her poem on the borderlands will conclude: "there in front of us is the crossroads and choice" (43). And she builds on the crossroads image's implications by arguing that this cultural rebellion ultimately represents not a betrayal nor even an abandonment of the initial culture, but rather a transformation that builds upon but transcends that starting point: "I was totally immersed *en lo mexicano.* . . . To separate from my culture (as from my family) I had to feel competent enough on the outside and secure enough inside to live life on my own. Yet in leaving home I did not lose touch with my origins because *lo mexicano* is in my system. I am a turtle, wherever I go I carry 'home' on my back" (43).

Anzaldúa lays out here an initial vision of the result of such transcendence and transformation, a preliminary and complex definition for the "new culture—*una cultura mestiza*" toward which this new community is moving. It constitutes, again, partly a rebellion against the more distinct and static cultures' values and perspectives, a rejection of "the myths of the tribe into which I was born"; at the same time, as the crossroads and turtle images suggest, a mestiza identity requires "an accounting with all three cultures—white, Mexican, Indian" and can ideally connect and mediate between those disparate but interconnected American communities. But mestiza identity comprises more than just response and relationship to existing cultures; as Anzaldúa traces in the chapter's lyrical concluding paragraphs, it more significantly involves the recognition and embrace of the many components of an alternative, hybrid culture: "the freedom to carve and chisel my own face" and "to fashion my own gods out of my entrails"; and the opportunity to "fight for her own skin and a piece of the ground to stand on, a ground from which to view the world—a perspective, a home ground where she can plumb the rich ancestral roots into her own ample *mestiza* heart" (43–45). As the shift in pronouns between those passages illustrates, Anzaldúa moves in this description, as in the chapter overall, from a more individual to a representative depiction of these experiences and this identity, making explicit the communal possibilities inherent in all the individual lives and narratives on which my book has focused.

Perhaps the most abstract phrase from those passages is "to fashion my own gods out of my entrails," and Anzaldúa turns in the next chapter, "Entering into the Serpent," to precisely the question of what a mestiza spirituality and mythology might comprise and symbolize. She acknowledges that she has a strong model for such hybrid spirituality in her family's cross-cultural religious beliefs and practices, the "folk Catholicism with many pagan elements" within which she was raised (49). And she dwells at length on two interconnected symbols that figure prominently in that folk Catholicism, although she unsurprisingly extends and deepens their alternative and mestiza meanings. The chapter's titular and overarching such symbol is the serpent, what Anzaldúa calls "*mi tono,* my animal counterpart." While that phrase suggests another very individual connection, Anzaldúa immediately adds a profoundly communal and mythological side to this symbol, noting that "like the ancient Olmecs, I know Earth is a coiled serpent" (48). She fleshes out that historical and cultural context, providing an extended, insider's ethnographic description of Coatlalopeuh, the goddess known as "She Who Has Dominion Over Serpents" who is, Anzaldúa notes, "the central deity connecting us [Chicanos] to our Indian ancestry" (49). But I would argue that the chapter's serpent imagery also serves two implicit but significant cross-cultural purposes: providing a mythological origin story that is quite literally alternative to the Christian book of Genesis, with the serpent's knowledge and perspective now that which we must remember and rediscover; and, more obliquely but relevantly, pointing to one of the foundational documents of American identity, Franklin's cartoon representation of the fledgling colonies as a divided snake who must "Join or Die." In light of the latter connection, Anzaldúa's narration of the Aztec culture's "splitting" of the goddess *Coatlalopeuh,* their "dividing her who had been complete" into opposing and warring elements (49), makes clear both the dangers of division and the promise if the serpent can be reunited by a mestiza culture that remembers and enters into her perspective.

If the serpent thus provides a significant spiritual and mythological context for a mestiza identity, Anzaldúa also analyzes in this chapter a more present and explicitly hybrid religious figure, the Virgin of Guadalupe. Anzaldúa portrays the Virgin as created by cross-cultural voices and stories on multiple levels: she provides a folk poem in Spanish that details the initial 1531 encounter between, as she subsequently glosses it, "Juan Diego, a poor Indian," and the Virgin, who "appeared [to him] on the spot where the Aztec goddess, *Tonantsi* ('Our Lady Mother'), had been worshipped by the Nahuas," and "speaking Nahuatl" tells Diego about her identity and role as "*María Coatlalopeuh*"; Anzaldúa then narrates the history of cross-cultural identifications and uses of the Virgin's image, first by "the Spanish . . . because *Coatlalopeuh* was homophonous to the Spanish Guadalupe," and then by multiple Mexican cultures and figures, including the Roman Catholic Church, the revolutionaries Emiliano Zapata and Miguel Hidalgo, striking migrant workers in the American Southwest, and "*pachucos* (zoot suiters) [who] tattoo her image on their bodies" (50–51). She links the Virgin's ongoing influence to her status as a "a synthesis of the old world and the new, of the religion and culture of the two races in our psyche"; the Virgin is "the symbol of the *mestizo,*" and as such she "unites people of different races, religions, languages, . . . mediates between the Spanish and Indian cultures (or three cultures in the case of *mexicanos* of African or other ancestry) and between Chicanos and the white world." And Anzaldúa takes that mediating role one step further, connecting it directly to first her own hybrid culture and then to all those individuals and communities defined by cross-cultural transformation: "*La Virgen de Guadalupe* is the symbol of ethnic identity and of the tolerance for ambiguity that Chicanos-*mexicanos,* people of mixed race, people who have Indian blood, people who cross cultures, by necessity possess" (52).

That "tolerance for ambiguity" represents, Anzaldúa elaborates in the chapter's particularly dense closing sections ("The Presences" and "*La facultad*"), a shift not only in communal understanding but also in an individual's perspective. In her case, she admits, that individual shift is partly grounded in "the gulf where I was raised," the literally cross-cultural "triangular piece of land wedged between the river *y el golfo* which serves as the Texas-U.S./Mexican border" (57). But she argues that every individual's upbringing both includes such cross-cultural origin points and yet comprises a kind of indoctrination against them, a series of lessons in what "we're not supposed to remember," the things "we're supposed to forget" in order to "accept . . . the 'official' reality of the rational, reasoning mode which is connected with external reality." Once again she works to create a hybrid alternative to that more stable and static vision, an argument for "the other modes of consciousness" based on the experiences of "people who inhabit both realities [and] are forced to live in the interface between the two, forced to become adept at switching modes" (58–59). It is this "shift in perception" that Anzaldúa names *la facultad,* and her most explicit definition of that faculty reflects both her images of the core that unites divided cultures and her book's own construction: "*La facultad* is the capacity to see in surface phenomena the meaning of deeper realities, to see the deep structure below the surface" (60–61). Just as Anzaldúa's sprawling book is unified by its construction of the many components of an alternative, hybrid American identity, so too are the distinct and seemingly divided cultures around which she has been raised ultimately connected through the deep structure of shared land and experience and future—and while *la facultad* is first a shift in individual perception about the world, it points toward the possibility for communities likewise to reframe their perspectives on the realities of history and identity.

Anzaldúa's next chapter, "*La herencia de Coatlicue/*The *Coatlicue* State," fleshes out the transformed state of consciousness that can result (for both individuals and communities) from *la facultad*'s shifts, and it does so first and foremost through the text's most striking and effective moment of hybridity. The chapter begins with an extremely free-form passage (I hesitate to call it something as traditional as a poem, although it resembles one) titled (or at least located under the words) "protean being"; it exemplifies that phrase not only by tracing the many changes in form and identity experienced by its female protagonist ("in the mirror she sees a woman with four heads"; "in the photograph a double image bisecting crisscrossing") but also in its own formal innovations (no punctuation or capitalization; elongated and seemingly random spacing; distinct words combined to create new ones such as "nightsky") (63–64). When Anzaldúa writes in the next section that "the mirror is an ambivalent symbol" (64), her words seem deeply metatextual, a description of how she will utilize this new textual form (which recurs later in the chapter) and its illustration of the *Coatlicue* State to represent the ambiguity of a mestiza perspective. Just as both a mirror and an experimental form of writing "can erect a barrier against the world" (64), so too does an individual with this new perspective feel "alien," "something deformed with evil inside," and "shame for being abnormal," suffer from a "fear that she has no names that she has many names that she doesn't know her names" (65). But just as "in a glance" at the mirror and the text "also lies awareness, knowledge" (64), so too can the individual come to understand and embrace her hybrid identity, the fact that "*mi cara, como la realidad, tenia un character multiplice* [my face, like reality, has a multiple character]" (66). So does her text, of course, never more than in this chapter, and that multiplicity reflects and comprises the realities of the alternative, transformative state for which she is arguing.

Just as the prior chapter ended with the most overt description of *la facultad*, Anzaldúa concludes this one by laying out in more traditionally narrated detail the cross-cultural meanings of the *Coatlicue* State. That state is, as one of the section headings makes explicit, "A Prelude to Crossing" (70), a necessary component to the perspective shift after which an embrace of cross-cultural transformation becomes both possible and ideal. It is, Anzaldúa acknowledges, a profoundly difficult and often painful place and process: "Every increment of consciousness, every step forward is a *travesía*, a crossing. I am again an alien in new territory. And again, and again. . . . 'Knowing' is painful because after 'it' happens I can't stay in the same place and be comfortable. I am no longer the same person I was before" (70). Much of that difficulty derives from the communal identities and histories from which any individual originates and which cannot be simply abandoned: "It hampers her movement in this new territory, dragging the ghost of the past with her" (71). But at the same time, the *Coatlicue* State represents once more a crossroads and a bridge, a way in which an individual can unite those distinct and divided cultures and move them forward into a new, hybrid identity: "Simultaneously, . . . she represents: duality in life, a synthesis of duality, and a third perspective—something more than mere duality or a synthesis of duality" (68). Whatever that third perspective is or can be, it is part of a new community, one connected to but not limited by—and in fact "something more than"—any of the existing communities: "Mine. Ours. Not the heterosexual white man's or the colored man's or the state's or the culture's or the religion's or the parents'—just ours, mine" (73).

Moving beyond those existing communities requires more than a shift in perspective, though, and Anzaldúa turns in the next chapter, "How to Tame a Wild Tongue," to one of the arenas in which cultures wield their most powerful influence: language. As she traces in the chapter's opening anecdotes, in her own life Anzaldúa has experienced cultural pressures on her use of language from two opposed yet similarly limiting perspectives: the pressure to speak English, whether from "the Anglo teacher" who noted that "if you want to be American, speak 'American.' If you don't like it, go back to Mexico where you belong," or from her mother, who was "mortified that I spoke English like a Mexican" and enrolled her in classes "to get rid of my accent" (75–76); and the pressure to resist those voices, as expressed by the "various Latinos and Latinas" who have called Anzaldúa a "*pocho,* cultural traitor, . . . speaking the oppressor's language by speaking English, . . . ruining the Spanish language" (77). Chicano Spanish, the hybrid language to which she has instead turned and in which her book is written, has been, she argues, similarly attacked, "considered by the purist and by most Latinos deficient, a mutilation of Spanish" (77), and the victim of "Linguistic Terrorism," not only through its categorizations from multiple cultural perspectives as "illegitimate, a bastard language" but also in the explicit (if ostensibly nonviolent) "repeated attacks" on those who speak it (80). Since "ethnic identity is twin skin to linguistic identity," those attacks are as much on an individual as they are on a community: "If you want to really hurt me," Anzaldúa notes, "talk badly about my language" (81).

Of all the components of a mestiza identity, however, it is this alternative language, and particularly its status as "a border tongue which developed naturally" and which remains "a living language" (77), that Anzaldúa is best equipped to defend, and she does so on three distinct but interconnected levels in this chapter. First, she breaks that language down in an ethnolinguistic way: creating a numbered list of "some of the languages we, [as] a complex heterogeneous people, speak" (77); describing and contextualizing the many situations in which she as an individual speaks these "tongues" (78); and providing linguistic analyses of the "significant differences in the Spanish we [Chicanos] speak," including the use of anglicisms and Tex-Mex elements (79–80). Second, she moves from these specific analyses to the language's broader cross-cultural contexts: she endeavors to trace its geographic diversity and trans-formations in order to prove that "Chicano Spanish is as diverse linguistically as it is regionally" (80–81), and she argues for using the language to create a personal narrative and identity, the way in which her ability and freedom "to write bilingually and to switch codes without having always to translate" links directly to her accep-tance of "the legitimacy of myself" and her belief that "I will have my voice: Indian, Spanish, white" (81). And third, she transitions from that reference to her own writing to a discussion of the exis-tence and value of an alternative, artistic and scholarly canon in this language; she links that canon to every level of her hybrid individual identity, from the cross-cultural music and movies of her childhood to her work "teaching High School English to Chicano students" and her inclusion of "Chicano literature [as] an area of focus" in her PhD studies (81–83). As with every one of her topics, there are moments in which this alternative canon seems directly opposed to the Anglo community, as when Anzaldúa writes in the chapter's final paragraph that "we [Chicanos] know what it is to live under the hammer blow of the dominant *norteamericano* culture" (85). But she has already complicated that question of cultural influences by highlighting the "kind of dual identity" that results from not "identify[ing] with the Anglo-American cultural values and [not] identify[ing] with the Mexican cultural values," and the chapter's final sentence drives home the hybrid culture comprised by that dual identity: "Stubborn, persevering, impenetrable as stone, yet possessing a malleability that renders us unbreakable, we, the *mestizas* and *mestizos,* will remain" (85–86).

Anzaldúa is more than just a reader or student of that cross-cultural canon, of course—she is also and most significantly the writer of an exemplary text within it, and in the next chapter, *"Tlilli, Tlapalli/*The Path of the Red and Black Ink," she steps back to analyze metatextually (as in the passage on her hybrid mosaic) her status and goals as such an alternative author. On one level, that status is a deeply individual and intimate one, a reflection of her "learning to live with *la Coatlicue.*" That process, which "transforms living in the Borderlands from a nightmare into a numinous experience, . . . is always a path/state to something else," and thus, Anzaldúa argues, "the painful periods of confusion that I suffer from are symptomatic of a larger creative process: cultural shifts. The stress of living with cultural ambiguity both compels me to write and blocks me" (95–96). Similarly, Anzaldúa defines the book's goals as on that individual level effecting a transformation in identity: "I write the myths in me, the myths I am, the myths I want to become" (93). But the individual and communal are as inseparable as ever here, and for a writer the former can profoundly influence the latter: "I am playing with my Self, I am playing with the world's soul, I am the dialogue between my Self and *el espiritu del mundo.* I change myself, I change the world" (92). In writing those myths of her self, then, Anzaldúa is at the same time helping to create and communicate new communal, American myths, in order to "root ourselves in the mythological soil and soul of this continent" (90). And in the passages that frame the chapter, Anzaldúa makes clear just how potently transformative this mestiza writer can be: she opens by arguing for "the ability of story (prose and poetry) to transform the storyteller and listener into something or someone else" and so for "the writer as shape-changer, . . . a *nahual,* a shaman" (88); and closes with a lyrical reiteration of that role's dangerous but vital hybridity and influence, her recognition "that the internal tension of oppositions can propel (if it doesn't tear apart) the *mestiza* writer out of the *metate* where she is being ground with corn and water, eject her out as *nahual,* an agent of transformation, able to modify and shape primordial energy and therefore able to change herself and others" (96–97).

If the penultimate prose chapter thus highlights Anzaldúa's broadest goals for her individual identity as a mestiza writer, then the concluding one, "*La conciencia de la mestiza/*Towards a New Consciousness," provides her broadest and most extended definition of the hybrid communal identity on which that writing is focused. The chapter's opening paragraph establishes many of that identity's ideal qualities and possibilities and is worth quoting in full:

> José Vasconcelos, Mexican philosopher, envisaged *una raza mestiza, una mezcla de razas afines, una raza de color—la primera raza síntesis del globo.* He called it a cosmic race, *la raza cosmica,* a fifth race embracing the four major races of the world. Opposite to the theory of the pure Aryan, and to the policy of racial purity that white America practices, his theory is one of inclusivity. At the confluence of two or more genetic streams, with chromosomes constantly "crossing over," this mixture of races, rather than resulting in an inferior being, provides hybrid progeny, a mutable, more malleable species with a rich gene pool. From this racial, ideological, cultural and biological cross-pollination, an "alien" consciousness is presently in the making—a new *mestiza* consciousness, *una conciencia de mujer.* It is a consciousness of the Borderlands. (99)

While Vasconcelos was, as Anzaldúa notes, imagining the broadest possible human community in developing this theory of inclusivity, there is a strikingly American context and connection operating just below the paragraph's surface. As she mentions in alluding to "the policy of racial purity" (although her attribution of it to "white America" is another moment in which she reifies rather than challenges cultural divisions), the fear of miscegenation, of racial mixture, has been a hugely instrumental element of American history; that fear has been directed most particularly and consistently at African Americans in the South, but has also been central to many of the nation's debates and controversies over the border, immigration, and the presence and influence of ethnic Americans of all races and nationalities. And as this paragraph makes clear, a vision of America with mestiza identity at the core is thus not just a bridge between divided cultures, nor even just a crossroads that can lead those cultures and the nation toward a new path—it offers a profound alternative to one of the nation's most pernicious traditional narratives, constructing an American history and identity founded on both the experience of crossing over and the hybrid progeny that are its most overt result.

As is the norm in her hybrid book, Anzaldúa shifts dramatically in focus, tone, and even genre immediately after that paragraph, into a poem about her very personal experiences as "a *mestiza* / continually walk[ing] out of one culture / and into another, / because I am in all cultures at the same time." She uses those experiences to balance the opening's idealism with her lived recognition of "the ambivalence" that is the result of "the clash of voices," her intimate awareness that "the *mestiza*'s dual or multiple personality is plagued by psychic restlessness" (99–100). Just as the cross-cultural experiences of my four prior focal figures often caused significant confusion and pain, so does "*la mestiza,* cradled in one culture, sandwiched between two cultures, straddling all three cultures and their value systems, undergo a struggle of flesh, a struggle of borders, an inner war. . . . The coming together of two self-consistent but habitually incompatible frames of reference" for such individuals, she admits, "causes *un choque,* a cultural collision." And just as each individual's cross-cultural experiences could at times produce a hardening of cultural divisions and hostilities, so too does Anzaldúa recognize that "subconsciously, we see an attack on ourselves and our beliefs as a threat and we attempt to block with a counterstance" (100). There is nothing simple or easy about this alternative identity for any individual confronted with it (not least because of the ongoing power of the original identities from which those individuals come), and of course any larger cross-cultural community would be comprised of and dependant on precisely such individuals.

Yet Anzaldúa has never offered simple or easy answers in her transformative text, instead both narrating and exemplifying what a complex, dense, mestiza identity can offer and mean. She does so for the remainder of this chapter as well, beginning with her rejection of the counterstance in favor of the argument that "at some point, on our way to a new consciousness, we will have to leave the opposite bank, the split between the two mortal combatants somehow healed so that we are on both shores at once" (100). The mestiza identity, she notes in the next section, has precisely the "tolerance for contradictions, a tolerance for ambiguity," concurrent to her "plural personality," that makes possible this movement "toward a more whole perspective, one that includes rather than excludes" (101). That move is especially vital because "the future, [which] depends on the straddling of two or more cultures, will belong to the *mestiza*." Far from simply representing a reaction to such change, the mestiza will be an instrument of it: "by creating a new mythos—that is, a change in the way we perceive reality, the way we see ourselves, and the ways we behave—*la mestiza* creates a new consciousness" (102). While the mestiza might thus seem, through the lens of traditional communities, "cultureless," Anzaldúa argues instead that "I am cultured because I am participating in the creation of yet another culture, a new story to explain the world and our participation in it, a new value system with images and symbols that connect us to each other. . . . *Soy un amasamiento,* I am an act of kneading, of uniting and joining. . . . I choose to use some of my energy to serve as mediator" (102–3, 107). And she represents those unifying and mediating roles once again through the image of a bridge, quoting a line of poetry by Gina Valdés: "Hay tantísimas fronteras / que dividen a la gente / pero por cada frontera / existe también un puente [There are so many borders / that divide the people, / but for each border / there exists also a bridge]" (107).

These final prose pages also both include and transcend two of the more limiting elements of Anzaldúa's ideas. There is, in the sense that this mestiza consciousness is something new, a seeming elision of—or at least distinct separation from—the past, as captured in Anzaldúa's description of "this step [as] a conscious rupture with all oppressive traditions of all cultures and religions" (104). Yet she later notes that the mestiza writer does not forget or avoid but rather "reinterprets history and, using new symbols, she shapes new myths" (105). The process, that is, is one of "seeing the Chicana anew in light of her history, . . . seek[ing] new images of identity, new beliefs about ourselves" through an awareness of but a refusal to remain chained to the past (109). Anzaldúa models an individual such revision in the chapter's final section, "*El retorno,*" as she returns to the valley in which she was raised and considers both its long history (including but extending well beyond her own familial heritage) and its evolving identity in the present. In her final two paragraphs she focuses more specifically still, on *"los Rosales de mama,"* the roses that have been a part of her family's relationship to this place for as long as they have been grounded there. These flowers symbolize, she writes in the chapter's last sentence, precisely the relationship to one's personal, familial, geographic, and cultural past that a re-vision implies: "A constant changing of forms, *renacimientos de la tierra madre* [rebirths of mother earth]" (112–13). The constant change is the history, at least in its ideal form, and the transformations rebirths of what remains most enduring and powerful in that cross-cultural past.

Also potentially limiting that cross-cultural identity, however, is the division between cultures that reappears at times in Anzaldúa's closing prose chapter. She opens one long paragraph, for example, by arguing that "individually, but also as a racial entity, we need to voice our needs. We need to say to white society: We need you to accept the fact that Chicanos are different, to acknowledge your rejection and negation of us"; the paragraph extends that first-person plural voice and communal identification (and its address but also opposition to a similarly communal second-person audience) to a litany of historical and cultural wrongs and claims. Yet as has been the case throughout the book, Anzaldúa abruptly and crucially undermines that sense of cultural division, ending the paragraph with a shift in the first-person pronoun's national emphasis and a concurrent plea to her fellow Americans to "admit that Mexico is your double, . . . that we are irrevocably tied to her. Gringo, accept the doppelganger in your psyche. By taking back your collective shadow the intra-cultural split will heal. And finally, tell us what you need from us" (107–8). As both the use of "intra" (rather than "inter") cultural and the final sentence's request for response and dialogue indicate, the American identity, past and future, being imagined here is one of connection and unity between these communities. And Anzaldúa once again uses the mestiza community both to exemplify that unified nation's fundamental shared core and to express a belief in that core's eventual recognition and embrace, noting, "We are a blending that proves that all blood is intricately woven together, and that we are spawned out of similar souls" (106–7).

In many ways the poems that constitute the second half of Anzaldúa's book move away from those symbols and arguments for a mestiza identity, tending instead to create relatively isolated images of the distinct cultures and communities to which Anzaldúa's individual identity connects. The poems in the section's first two chapters, for example, mostly depict the divisions and hostile relationship between the Chicano and Anglo communities: those in chapter 1, "*Mas antes en los ranchos* [Earlier on the Ranches]," highlight historical divisions related to prejudice and violence; while those in chapter 2, "*La perdida* [The Loss]," emphasize the difficulties and dangers of illegal immigration and migrant labor. Reflecting the extreme and negative cultural attitudes in both directions are the titles of two poems in "*La perdida*": "*El sonavabitche*" refers to a brutal white employer to whose inhumane treatment the poem's Chicano speaker finally stands up (146–51); while in "We Call Them Greasers" Anzaldúa creates the perspective of such an inhumane white rancher, as he describes his and his men's dispossession, rape, and lynching of a Chicano family (156–57). Chapters 3, 4, and 5 shift the tone and emphasis to more positive communal identifications and connections—gay and lesbian sexuality in chapter 3, "Crossers *y otros atravesados*"; women's experiences and lives in chapter 4, "*Cihuatlyotl*, Woman Alone"; and Indian mythology and identity in chapter 5, "*Animas*"—but still portray those communities as largely distinct, both from their respective opposed communities and from each other. Illustrating the respective insularity of such communal identifications are the dedications of chapter 3's "*Compañera, cuando amabamos*" to "other spik dykes" (168–69) and chapter 4's "*En el nombre de todas las madres* [In the name of all the mothers]" to that entirely gendered group (182–85).These poems, like the others in these chapters, are complex and meaningful (in both form and theme) in their own right, but they feel somewhat discontinuous with much of what has come before, particularly the final prose chapter's thorough development and embrace of a cross-cultural, unifying mestiza community.

Yet the book's poetic half does also comprise a continuing engagement with that mestiza ideal, on both a formal and, ultimately, a thematic level. Formally, Anzaldúa's inclusion of a poetic half in her personal narrative, the book that speaks of her existence, extends and deepens a trend that has been evident in all my texts: that the personal narrative, like the cross-cultural identity to which it connects, contains multitudes, expands to encompass the many roles and communities that comprise its subject's transformative life. Cabeza de Vaca's exploration chronicle becomes an ethnography and account of his decade of travels across the New World; Rowlandson's captivity narrative includes glimpses of both the historical contexts of King Philip's War and the social and economic structures of the Wampanoag tribe; Equiano's interesting life story vacillates between observations of slavery's horrors and detailed descriptions of the worlds of naval and merchant ships; Winnemucca's account of her tribe's wrongs and claims also documents her family's multigenerational cross-cultural vision and her own trajectory toward a mediating interpreter's role. In this light, Anzaldúa's hybrid text, like her mestiza identity, becomes only a particularly overt and visible late-twentieth-century representation of experiences and lives that have been central to America throughout the five centuries since the first European-native encounters. Her ability to include and—most relevantly—publish such generic and cultural hybridity directly relates to the contemporary trends toward ethnic studies and multiculturalism, both in and out of academia; but while those movements would focus more on the distinct communities that the first five chapters of poetry represent (Chicano studies, gay and lesbian studies, women's studies, Native American studies), it is precisely the hybridity itself that comprises the core of Anzaldúa's text and identity.

Moreover, the title of the sixth and final poetic chapter, "*El retorno,*" denotes not only the mestiza return to a Southwestern homeland but also, and more importantly, the text's return to an emphasis on that hybrid, mestiza identity. That return is introduced subtly in the chapter's first poem, "*Arriba mi gente* [Arise my people]"; the poem is written largely in Spanish and thus might seem directed solely at Chicanos, but the first four lines, which Anzaldúa calls the "Chorus" and which are repeated four times in the poem, point in a different direction, both linguistically and communally: "*Arriba mi gente, / toda gente arriba* / In spirit as one, / all people arising" (214–15). As both the lines' multilingualism and their images of unity and inclusiveness indicate, the community of "my people" here seems closely tied to Vasconcelos' concept of an inclusive, hybrid race, one that knows (or at least stops at) no cultural or linguistic borders. The next poem, the aforementioned "To live in the Borderlands means you," reinforces that border-crossing hybridity, particularly in its closing invocation of the crossroads image. And the chapter and book's final poem—or rather two poems, as Anzaldúa provides both a Spanish and English version, extending the previous chorus's multilingual reach—makes an explicit argument for the ideal, hybrid future that lies beyond that crossroads. That poem, "Don't Give In, *Chicanita*," is dedicated to Anzaldúa's niece Missy; the dedication represents the book's first reference to Missy (despite Anzaldúa's extended discussions of her family, past and present), turning the focus to the next generation in a clear and striking way. The poem's six stanzas are evenly divided between an argument for the value of remembering and embracing a mestiza past (the first three stanzas) and a belief in an ideal communal future (the last three). After opening with a plea to Missy to "endure," Anzaldúa notes, "Your lineage is ancient, / your roots like those of the mesquite / firmly planted, digging underground / toward that current, the soul of *tierra madre*—/ your origin." She later makes explicit the connection between endurance and history, comparing "us" to "the horned toad and the lizard / relics of an earlier age." But that past has also been transformed, and so in the future "we'll be members of a new species / . . . And alive *m'ijita*, very much alive." Indeed, the final stanza concludes, that future will belong to this cross-cultural, mestiza community: "Yes, in a few years or centuries / *la Raza* will rise up, tongue intact / carrying the best of all the cultures. . . . You'll see" (224–25).

Like Maxine Hong Kingston before her, Anzaldúa recognizes the crucial value of remembering and engaging with, and then communicating to both fellow community members and outsiders, one's cultural heritage and identity. In that series of interconnected goals, both women's texts fall in line with the trends of identity politics, ethnic studies, and multiculturalism that dominated much of American culture in the late twentieth century. But as Kingston captures in her second book, particularly in its portrayal of her father's experiences and life, American history and identity do not break down so easily into distinct cultures—or rather, those distinct cultures are transformed in and by America into something hybrid and cross-cultural. At its heart Anzaldúa's hybrid mosaic of a text both thematizes and embodies that cross-cultural, mestiza American core, portraying the alternative history, culture, spirituality and mythology, language and canon and writing, and community that constitute such a mestiza identity. Her explicit goal in creating such a text is not only to add that mestiza community to the mix but to allow it to serve as a bridge between divided cultures and, more important still, a crossroads to a more unified and truly communal American future. If she, as the subject and author of her personal narrative, is both the illustration and the agent of that transformation, then the next generation, like Missy Anzaldúa, is its descendent, the inheritor of this complex and evolving cross-cultural American legacy. And as America has moved into the early twenty-first century, we have for the first time elected to our highest political office a man who is likewise overtly and unmistakably a descendant of cross-cultural transformation: Barack Hussein Obama, to whose personal narrative and identity I turn in my conclusion.

Conclusion

Electing Transformation

For proponents of both the multicultural and traditional narratives of American history, the presidential campaign, election, and early presidency of Barack Hussein Obama have provided ample opportunities to reiterate and reify their perspectives. From the multicultural side, perhaps the single most salient such moment is John Lewis's Inauguration Day remark to journalist David Remnick that "Barack Obama is what comes at the end of that bridge in Selma," an image that seeks at once to remind Americans of the dark history of racial segregation and violence and to argue for the significance and eventual triumph of the Civil Rights movement.[1] Yet equally multicultural in their connections of an individual to a specific and singular racial identity were Jesse Jackson's repeated critiques of candidate Obama for (among other similar failings) "acting like he's white." Many of the more famous and controversial critiques of President Obama from the traditional side seem to align closely with parallel and ongoing criticisms of multicultural America: these include Glenn Beck's characterization of Obama as "a racist" who has a "deep-seated hatred of white people," Rush Limbaugh's argument that the health care reform bill represents a form of "reparations," and numerous descriptions of Sonia Sotomayor as an "affirmative action pick" for the Supreme Court.[2] Moreover, I have argued throughout this book that both narratives centrally construct racial and ethnic identities in explicit and static terms, and in this vein Obama's own self-identification on the 2010 Census as "black" has validated the frequent celebrations (on one extreme) of his status as "the first black President" and (on the other extreme) the racial slurs and attacks that have come to be associated with many of the protests against his administration and policies.[3]

While many of these narratives had been connected to Obama since his earliest emergence onto the national political scene, they perhaps began to crystallize around the Reverend Wright controversy in early 2008, particularly in response to Obama's "More Perfect Union" speech in March of that year. After all, the speech provided striking evidence on which proponents of each narrative could focus to make their case for Obama as illustrative of their perspective. Obama's extended meditation on "the history of racial injustice in this country," and more precisely on the legacies of slavery and segregation and their ongoing relevance for the African American community and thus churches such as Wright's Trinity, coupled with his closing exhortation to all Americans to move beyond racial divisions and embody the Founders' vision of a more perfect union, led naturally to multicultural celebrations of the speech as a fitting heir to the orations of Frederick Douglass and (especially) Martin Luther King Jr.[4] For traditionalists, on the other hand, Obama's decision to "throw his white grandmother under the bus" by acknowledging her "fear of black men who passed her by on the street" and her tendency to "utter racial or ethnic stereotypes that made me cringe" reflected his overt and divisive racial identity politics and made clear that he was Reverend Wright's heir as well as his parishioner.[5]

Yet the reference to Obama's "white grandmother" (as he calls her in that paragraph) serves as an overt reminder that the voice and identity behind this speech are not simply or fundamentally African American but instead mixed and multiracial at their core, the product of cross-cultural transformations across multiple generations. Obama engages directly with that cross-cultural heritage in the speech's sixth and seventh paragraphs, its first discussion of his own identity and perspective, making that heritage both formally and thematically the foundation for everything that follows. As he argues there, his belief that all Americans "want to move in the same direction" comes not only from his "unyielding faith in the decency and generosity of the American people" but also from his "own American story." As he delineates that story,

I am the son of a black man from Kenya and a white woman from Kansas. I was raised with the help of a white grandfather who survived a Depression to serve in Patton's Army during World War II and a white grandmother who worked on a bomber assembly line at Fort Leavenworth while he was overseas. I've gone to some of the best schools in America and lived in one of the world's poorest nations. I am married to a black American who carries within her the blood of slaves and slaveowners—an inheritance we pass on to our two precious daughters. I have brothers, sisters, nieces, nephews, uncles and cousins, of every race and every hue, scattered across three continents, and for as long as I live, I will never forget that in no other country on Earth is my story even possible.

It's a story that hasn't made me the most conventional candidate. But it is a story that has seared into my genetic makeup the idea that this nation is more than the sum of its parts—that out of many, we are truly one.

In the second paragraph in particular, Obama seeks not only to define his own ongoing identity as intimately connected to this heritage of cross-cultural transformation but also, and more significantly, to link that heritage directly to his vision of American identity at its most fundamental level; the second sentence's slippage from his individual "genetic makeup" to the nation's constitution is, I believe, precisely Obama's point. In that light, the speech's closing appeal for a collective move toward a more perfect union becomes something more than just a bridging of the gaps between distinct racial or ethnic communities; "it is where we start" and "where our union grows stronger," Obama argues, and while the specific referent for that "it" is the now-famous story of an elderly black activist who has come to work for the campaign because of a young white one ("I'm here because of Ashley," the man notes), the broader meaning is the heritage of cross-cultural transformation to which both of those individuals, like Obama himself, are the heirs.

If the "More Perfect Union" speech is thus structured by Obama's analyses of his own and the nation's heritage of cross-cultural transformation, his first and best book, and fullest personal narrative to date, *Dreams from My Father: A Story of Race and Inheritance* (1995), explicitly and profoundly focuses on such transformations on two key levels. Much of the book represents an extended and complex engagement with the cross-cultural transformations experienced by Obama's father and mother; as the title suggests and as Obama acknowledges in the preface to the book's second (2004) edition, his father's more overt and dramatic transformations are the text's principal subject (and will be my primary interest here), but I believe that his mother's own transformations are equally meaningful and illustrative and that they do make their way into the book as well (if in more subtle and partial ways).[6] And the purpose for that engagement is Obama's awareness of his own status as the descendent of those two lives and cross-cultural transformations, a status that makes both him and his multigenerational and yet intimate and self-reflective narrative powerfully representative of and illuminating for America's identity and future in the early twenty-first century.

Given the basic facts of Obama's family, it might seem like a serious stretch to say that Obama could know much at all, much less write a personal narrative, about the elder Barack.[7] After his parents separated and his father returned to Kenya (when Obama was two), Obama interacted with his father only for a single (certainly important but nonetheless brief) month, at the age of ten. Thus, other than his name and half of his racial identity (no small details, to be sure, but not ones that could tell him much in a specific sense about his father), Obama could be said to know, even to have inherited, very little about and from his dad. Moreover, the book's first two parts explicitly focus on both Obama's life and those family members and close friends with whom he was actually surrounded: "Origins" describes his childhood growing up with his single mother and her parents, and then his teenage peers, in Hawaii; while "Chicago" narrates the causes and effects of his postcollege decision to leave New York and become a community organizer in that city. "Kenya," the book's third and final section, does narrate a long trip Obama takes to his father's native land before his matriculation at Harvard Law School, but that section too centers very fully on Obama's journey and how it impacts his individual perspective and identity.

Despite these biographical facts and narrative emphases, however, Obama's book, like (he argues both implicitly and explicitly throughout) his life, is quite strikingly structured around his father. Partly that is due precisely to his father's absence, and the questions and searches that it produced and continues to produce in Obama (and that, again, lead him at times in this narrative to minimize his overt engagement with his mother's more consistent and practical role in his life; she does, however, represent his most full connection to his father, and so in that way her voice becomes as central to his text as her influence was to his life). But the book highlights a more positive set of paternal influences as well: the ways in which Barack's voice and identity and, perhaps especially, his cross-cultural experiences remain present and significant for Obama at each stage of his life, with each textual section introducing and analyzing his father's presence in Obama's book and identity.

In the first section, that presence arises predominantly through the many stories told to the young Obama of his father, and specifically of what Barack's cross-cultural experiences symbolized for those in Hawaii who knew him best (Obama's mother and grandparents, but also other Hawaiian friends). The most oft-repeated such story is, not coincidentally, the most symbolic and American: a barroom confrontation between Barack (the only black in a bar full of locals) and a racist Hawaiian who complains about having to drink "next to a nigger." The story highlights Barack's ability to change even such deep-seated prejudices, explicitly through the smiling lecture he delivers to the man on "the folly of bigotry [and] the promise of the American dream" (after which they drink together), but implicitly through the way his own experiences with and representation of that promise prove the bigotry false. The story was repeated so often, Obama believes, because it "captured the essence of the morality tale that my father's life had become," and the lessons it conveys, like the unique life it illustrates, are both thoroughly cross-cultural and profoundly American (10–11).

This part of the text includes Obama's one actual encounter with his father, that month-long visit during the Christmas season in his tenth year, but Obama frames that section with two distinct but interconnected kinds of stories. Before narrating the visit, Obama returns to the still-prominent yet "incomplete" stories of Barack that his mother has continued to tell him over the years. There is something uneasy for the young Obama about those stories, and more exactly about the complex "image" of his father that they have produced for him, "something unknown, something volatile and vaguely threatening" (63). Yet those uncertainties also produce in Obama a desire to learn more about this part of his heritage, leading for example to a trip to the nearby public library to research and read about his father's tribe, the Luo. And it is far from coincidental that the piece of information that most "spark[s] my interest" is a detail of the tribe's historical transformations, the fact that they "were a Nilotic people who had migrated to Kenya from their original home along the banks of the world's greatest river" (64). Having already in his first decade of life moved with his mother to Indonesia (she has remarried, to an Indonesian, and begun a new life there) and then back to Hawaii to live with his grandparents once more, Obama has inaugurated his own cross-cultural experiences and transformations, and perhaps can begin to appreciate more fully the significance of such journeys in both his family's and father's pasts as a result.

The month with his father passes quickly and without any overt revelations for Obama about the man or his past, but at the end of the visit, and likewise the end of the chapter that depicts it, Obama narrates another, much more personal and affecting, story of his father. The story concerns a Kenyan dance that Barack performs for and then with his son on "the day of his departure," a last effort to share with Obama "the sounds of your continent" before he returns to that distant homeland. Barack's performance represents the text's fullest moment of familial connection for Obama, as first his father's "solemn face spread[s] into a silly grin," then his "mother smile[s]," and finally his "grandparents walk in to see what all the commotion [is] about." Even more meaningfully, the dance climaxes first with the young Obama hesitantly joining in, taking his "first tentative steps" to emulate his father, and then with Barack's jubilant response, his voice raised in "a shout that leaves much behind and reaches out for more"; the moment and voice have clearly stayed with Obama long after that month's conclusion and his father's departure and redisappearance from his life (70–71). This latter framing story thus illustrates how much Barack's cross-cultural identity and heritage continued to evolve, not only in his own life (since this shared performance clearly had great meaning for him as well as for his son) but also in Obama's developing understanding: a maturing perspective that depends both on learning about the past of his father and paternal family (as the library trip indicates), and on reflecting on what it means to descend from them as well as from the mother and grandparents in whose home the performance occurred.

Although the book's first section ends by coming full circle to where it began, with the 21–year-old Obama learning that his father's journey has ended with his death in a car accident in Kenya, the repetition includes an addition that highlights how much the stories of his father have contributed to Obama's own evolution across his first two decades of life. Obama follows this second narration of the phone call with a deeply symbolic dream that reveals how fully his father's voice and presence have remained with him: Obama visits his father in a Kenyan prison cell, and when his father remarks with surprise on how thin his son has gotten, Obama responds that "if I was thin it was only because I took after him." On an emotional level, the dream perhaps provides some of the closure that Obama has not been able to achieve with his father, as he imagines his father saying that he has "always wanted to tell you how much I love you." But even more significantly, it helps him understand those complex but influential ways in which his relationship with his father remains open and evolving: upon waking he realizes more than ever before how much his father's experiences and identity have shaped his own, "how even in his absence his strong image had given me some bulwark on which to grow up, an image to live up to, or disappoint." And he likewise realizes that his engagement with his father's cross-cultural identity and life must continue, that he "need[s] to search for him . . . and talk with him again" (128–29).

I'll move more quickly through the narrative's subsequent two sections, although each includes his father, and more precisely Obama's ongoing engagement with his father's cross-cultural identity and life, in similarly complex and crucial formal and thematic ways. In the second section, "Chicago," Obama again frames a deeply personal and individual subject—his decision to work as a community organizer and his experiences in that role—with connections to his father; here those connections comprise his first visits and conversations with two of Barack's other children, Obama's half-sister Auma and half-brother Roy. It is Auma's stories of Barack and Kenya—Obama cedes a significant portion of text to her voice here, as she tells Obama everything she can "remember . . . about the Old Man" and through him about her own young life and identity (212)—that directly contribute to his decision to leave a prestigious New York law firm and become a community organizer. Auma helps Obama understand that the only genuine guidance he can receive from his father, "all he could tell" Obama, is "what had happened to him"; he admits that those transformative experiences were in his father's case partly a model of an incomplete life, and so could lead him to "the same defeat that had brought down the Old Man," but also recognizes that this "newfound liberation," if joined with the kind of continued exploration of the past and himself that a trip to Kenya (with Auma's suggestion of which the moment and chapter ends) could provide, can produce a life in which the past influences but does not circumscribe the present and future (221–22).

Having come to that new understanding, Obama's most immediate choice is to become a full-time community organizer in Chicago. His more painful and partial connection to the section's other new family member, his half-brother Roy, both challenges and reinforces the convictions he begins to develop through that work. Roy's "memories of the Old Man" are darker than Auma's, and represent for Obama another side to his own self-understanding, one that is "more immediate, more taunting," in which "the past remain[s] an open sore" (265). Roy's voice thus reminds Obama, as do some of Obama's most difficult experiences with troubled young men in Chicago, that he still has much to learn, and that his transformative experiences have in some ways led him "into [a] different tribe, speaking a different tongue, living by a different code" than these men (271). Yet his encounters with Roy also reiterate Obama's developing faith in a cross-cultural community that can cut across such differences and reinforce his belief that, as he tells Roy, "you don't have to do it alone.... We can share the load" (267). It is worth highlighting that both of these young Kenyan American relatives of Obama's are experiencing their own ongoing, difficult, and yet crucial cross-cultural transformations, so that his encounters with them not only amplify his multifaceted connections to his father's past but also strengthen his sense of this defining American experience as it continues to evolve for multiple individuals (and communities) in the present.

The third section, "Kenya," focused as it is on Obama's long journey to and through that African nation, is particularly connected to his father. Obama ends the section's opening chapter with a paragraph detailing all the places in Kenya where he feels his "father's presence, . . . asking [him] to understand," and the whole section extends directly from that moment and request (323). The second section's inclusion of Auma's and Roy's voices and perspectives is also extended and deepened here, as Obama transcribes 29 pages of his paternal grandmother's voice, narrating their family's and especially Barack's story. The section culminates in a somewhat melodramatic but deeply affecting internal dialogue between Obama and Barack, as the son stands by his father's grave and contemplates his inheritances, literal (he has just received the few possessions his father left him) and figurative. Moreover, both his grandmother's story and his graveside conversation emphasize the promise and pain of his father's multiple cross-cultural transformations, his journeys first within Kenya (such as his move away from his own father's Islamic faith), then to America, and then back to Kenya again. Such journeys, Obama can now see, do not mean breaking from the past or creating a fully individual identity, for "after seeming to travel so far," his father came to "discover that he had not escaped at all, . . . that he remained trapped on his father's island." Instead, his father's cross-cultural journeys, like his own that have led him back to Kenya as much as forward to Chicago, are at their ideal core about communal connection, the embrace of "a faith that wasn't new, that wasn't black or white or Christian or Muslim but that pulsed in the heart of the first African village and the first Kansas homestead—a faith in other people." While there is a universal human quality to that understanding, there is also for Obama a specifically American side to it; the section concludes with his realization that his "life in America" is fully "connected with this small plot of earth an ocean away," that his "birthright," what he has inherited above all, is each stage and meaning of his father's and family's identity and experiences (428–30).

Obama ends his book with an epilogue about his wedding, an event that symbolizes the many ways in which such realizations and connections will continue into his American life and future (not least through his own role as father to two young girls, about whom he writes at moments throughout the book and whose existence is of course foreshadowed through his marriage to Michelle). Significantly, he devotes much of this epilogue to his half-brother Roy, whose cross-cultural transformations continue to be particularly complicated but have become decidedly more optimistic. Roy has converted to Islam and now goes by the Kenyan name "Abongo," but also gains at the ceremony "two new mothers" in Obama's mother and maternal grandmother. In this very mixed identity, one that is "not without tension" but that "has given him solid ground to stand on" and "a pride in his place in the world," Abongo both mirrors Obama and yet has found his own, even more overtly cross-cultural American identity, one that, Obama admits, makes him "proudest of all." And Abongo's wedding toast, "To those who are not here with us," with which Obama ends his book, brings their father into the text one final and especially poignant time, and makes clear how much Barack's transformative experiences remain influential in his children's present and future identities and perspectives (440–42).

Important as that wedding is to Obama's life and narrative, I want to end by analyzing at greater length the event with which I began this conclusion, one even more explicitly connected to the future and with broader national meaning (and just as much personal meaning to Obama): the 2008 presidential campaign and election. In July 2008, responding generally to Obama's first (as a presidential candidate), much-heralded trip to Europe and specifically to his recommendation that Americans could benefit from emulating Europeans' knowledge of multiple languages, Mitt Romney argued that "Barack Obama looks towards Europe for a lot of his inspiration. John McCain is going to make sure that America stays America."[8] Of the many things that were at stake in this election and remain crucial in its aftermath, I believe that none is more far-reaching than the question of how we define America; and more exactly, of whether we see Obama—and not just his inspirations and views and ideas, and now his administration's policies, but also and more meaningfully still his names, his heritage, his identity—as profoundly American or vaguely, overtly, or even threateningly un- or anti-American.

Arguments for the latter position became increasingly prominent over the campaign's closing months, and have come to dominate much of the opposition to Obama's presidency. They appeared first in various corners of the right-wing media and blogosphere, as exemplified by a September 2008 web post titled "Alien Obama" by the blogger Confederate Yankee; he first cites an anti-Obama article by University of Oklahoma Professor David Deming, an overt proponent of the traditional narrative known for his opposition to academic multiculturalism, and then argues, "Barack Obama despises America and American values because he has never known or experienced them, as he did not grow up in a normal American culture . . . he is un-American. Our cultural memory and experiences are something he read about in books, but never lived, and something he cannot feel. He is not one of us." Such arguments emerged more and more overtly in McCain and Palin's culminating campaign speeches and events, most especially in their shared and repeated question "Who is the real Barack Obama?" and in some of the crowd responses caught on tape, which included "Terrorist" and "Traitor."[9] The arguments' effects could be seen not only in the insulated audiences for those speeches but in the responses of Americans across the nation and political spectrum, as illustrated by an October 2008 *Los Angeles Times* story about a Virginia couple who were lifelong Democrats but who noted, in response to a Democratic organizer's efforts to secure their vote, that they didn't believe they'd be able to vote for Obama, as he "just doesn't seem like he's from America" (Wallsten). And this narrative's contents and effects are concisely encapsulated in the title of an October 2008 *Time* cover story (ostensibly analyzing such responses to Obama, but also contributing to them far more than would have been possible with any other candidate): "Is Barack Obama American Enough?" (Beinert).

Despite Obama's clear victory over McCain at the polls, this narrative of his un-Americanness has of course continued into and even gained in force and prominence over the first two years of his presidency. It has provided the driving force behind any number of striking and singular controversies, such as the opposition to his September 2009 back-to-school speech; many other presidents (including Republicans Ronald Reagan and George H. W. Bush) gave such addresses to schoolchildren, but when Obama announced his plans to do so, it led the chairman of the Florida Republican Party to argue that he was going "against beliefs of the majority of Americans, while bypassing American parents through an invasive abuse of power."[10] But nothing exemplifies this narrative more than the Birther movement, the relatively small but extremely vocal and animated community of Americans (including at least a few members of Congress) who believe (despite clear and indisputable evidence to the contrary) that Obama was born outside of the United States and thus is constitutionally ineligible to serve as President.[11] Given that

John McCain himself was born in Panama (in the Panama Canal territory, part of the United States at the time) and yet was the subject of no such prominent controversy, the Birther movement represents without question a response to elements of Obama's identity and life that directly challenge certain traditional narratives and definitions of America. That perspective is embodied most concisely by the woman who famously tied questions about Obama's birth certificate, at her congressman's August 2009 Town Hall meeting, to her plaintive cry of "I want my country back!" (Roof).

There are many different ways to argue for the opposite position, to highlight how much more American Obama's story is than perhaps any prior presidential candidate's. But in the context of this project, and remembering how Obama himself addressed that question in his "More Perfect Union" speech, I would argue that it is as a descendant of and heir to cross-cultural transformations—and certainly of two such transformations, since his mother, through marrying the elder Barack and then raising the younger one, along with her subsequent second marriage to an Indonesian man, her years living with him in Indonesia, the daughter she had with him, and so on, experienced many such shifts herself—that Obama most fully reflects and represents and speaks for all twenty-first-century Americans. His parents' transformations were perhaps more dramatic, and certainly his father's more transient, than most (as can likewise be said of my chapters' focal individuals in one way or another); but they, and just as importantly the questions and searches, pains and promises, communal and familial and individual identities that they bequeathed to their son, are nonetheless exemplary of foundational American identities and experiences, of the cross-cultural shifts that have constituted this nation from its origins.

I can't say that, and can't conclude this book, without mentioning at least briefly some of the manifold ways in which I'm implicated in that idea as well. There is for example my Mom's American family: her grandparents born in Jewish villages in Eastern Europe and chased away by the pogroms; her parents born in Massachusetts shortly after their families' immigrations and moving between more and less orthodox Jewish identities and worlds throughout their lives, including her Dad's military service in World War II and her Mom's psychological and emotional return to childhood in her final years because of Alzheimer's; her marriage to a non-Jew, the descendent of Germans from Missouri on his mother's side and British-Canadians from New Hampshire on his father's; together their raising two children in Virginia with little explicit emphasis on that Jewish heritage; and her work in the Bright Stars program with impoverished and even homeless American children of literally dozens of different ethnic and national heritages (and languages), children who are a part of our national identity and future that we all too often ignore.

Then there is my wife's American family: her parents born in northern China, her father in a very rural village into extreme poverty and her mother in the province's capital to a government official and so into relative wealth; both in their teens chased to Taiwan by the Communist revolution, meeting and marrying there, and coming to America after college (with a brief stay in Belgium for her Mom on the way, at least in part because the Immigration and Nationality Act of 1965 had not yet made it possible for her immigrate to America); my wife being educated first in Chinese preschool classes and programs and then American public schools, speaking principally Mandarin at home and with her parents (into her adulthood) but only English with her Caucasian husband and their two boys.

And finally there are those two boys, my sons, and their American identities: growing up half Chinese and a quarter Jewish and a quarter English-German American; with the last name Railton but the name Tsao as a second middle name; with grandparents who speak Mandarin and grandparents who speak English; and perhaps most of all with so many questions, potentially difficult and (I hope with all my heart) potentially liberating, about who they'll be as they grow up. As Obama's epilogue intimates, if we start (as our narratives and identities always do) with the dreams from our fathers and mothers, we have to end with the dreams for our kids, and it's there in particular that the stakes of these conversations and of my project truly exist.

So what do my kids share with those other individuals and stories from my extended family, and with Obama and his parents, and with the protagonists of each of my book's chapters and narratives? What unifies such disparate and divided identities and experiences?

America, and more specifically the way such cross-cultural transformations have always been central to the individuals and families and communities and cultures that have come here and lived
here and constituted "here". That's the history from which we're all
descended, that's all of our American inheritance, and that's what
Obama truly represents, more overtly and visibly than perhaps any
prominent American before him. He could be, in a purely symbolic
but deeply meaningful sense, the first American president. And just
as we elected transformation in November 2008, so too, I believe,
can we elect to redefine America, to embrace the heritage of cross-
cultural transformation that he embodies and we all share.

Notes

Preface

1. My brief account here does not by any means cover all of the case's complexities and disputed details.
2. Springsteen's song was perceived by the New York police as a direct attack, with the head of the state's Fraternal Order of Police calling the artist a "fucking dirtbag" and the Patrolmen's Benevolent Association calling for a boycott. See Boehlert. Such responses are, to my mind, far more illustrative of the divisions in perspective I outlined at the beginning of this preface than of the specifics of Springsteen's song, sympathetic as its first verse unquestionably is to the police officers' situation.

Introduction

1. Similarly, the debates that have received the most attention in the early twenty-first century, those over abortion and gay rights, are often if not always connected to and driven by these differing perspectives on religion (specifically evangelical Christianity) in American history, culture, and identity.
2. Nash's textbook *Red, White, and Black: The Peoples of Early North America* (first published in 1974 and now in its sixth edition), likely the text to which Newfield and Gordon are most directly responding here, represents a definite (if more specific and historically focused) model for my project's ideas and readings.
3. This hemispheric definition of a cross-cultural America puts me in conversation with one of the region's most significant and impressive scholarly voices, Edouard Glissant. In "Creolization in the Making of the Americas," for example, Glissant argues that it was precisely such cross-cultural processes and "the extraordinary complexity of the exchanges between cultures" (275) that produced the new world's foundational identity.
4. It would be possible to trace America's origins back to the Native American cultures and nations that were present before European contact, in which case this element of my argument might be less plausible (although one could argue, as Gloria Anzaldúa does, that there were transformations within and

across those native cultures). But to my mind, America originates in the late fifteenth- and early sixteenth-century initial encounters between European and Native Americans, and it is to that point of origin that I refer here.

5. As Grobman notes, both Young, in her emphasis on the "heterogeneity and interspersion of groups" and how they "move within social processes that involve considerable exchange, interaction, and interdependency among the groups," (18–20) and Bhabha, in his concept of hybridity as "a cultural mixing resulting in something new," (21) offer philosophical and theoretical (albeit not specifically Americanist or historicist in any extended sense) underpinnings for projects like these and mine.

6. For a recent work that expressly emphasizes and celebrates the genre's interdisciplinarity, see McGovern.

Chapter 1

1. For an impressive example of what kind of histories of the era this new perspective can produce, see Sokolow.

2. In keeping with general scholarly practice, I refer to Cabeza de Vaca by "de Vaca" (rather than simply "Vaca") throughout this chapter.

3. De Vaca uses the formal "*obligar*," which could even be translated as "to force" rather than "to oblige," here. While I read the *Narrative* in an English translation, I also consulted the original Spanish in every case such as this one, where the specific word choice or grammar is critical to my analysis.

Chapter 2

1. See also Kupperman, *Settling with the Indians* and *Indians and English*.

2. For arguments that such opposed and often hostile cultural relationships were crucial to the construction of European American identity over the next century, see Shoemaker and also Silver.

3. According to the Julian calendar, still in use in Rowlandson's era, March 25 marked the beginning of a new year. So from her perspective, February was still part of 1675, whereas in our own reckoning—having shifted to the Gregorian calendar—it would be part of 1676. See Klekowski.

4. See also Burnham, and Goodman.

5. For a recent, more cross-cultural analysis of Rowlandson's narrative and New World religious identities, see Dillon.

6. Rowlandson divides her text not into chapters but into "Removes," with each constituting a shift to a new location in her journey.

Chapter 3

1. Wheatley does note here the entirely negative effects of slavery on the parents from whom such "babe[s] belov'd" are taken, connecting that communal and multi-generational experience to her individual hope that "others may never feel tyrannic sway."

2. Jefferson, "The Declaration of Independence." Edmund Morgan's *American Slavery, American Freedom: The Ordeal of Colonial Virginia* remains the definitive analysis of the interconnections between these seemingly contradictory facets of Revolutionary America.

3. For an extended analysis of African Americans (including Wheatley and Equiano) and the Revolution, see Egerton; for broader arguments about African (and all) Americans and cross-cultural identities in the period, see Sobel and Gilroy. For a contrasting perspective on class and racial divisions in Revolutionary Virginia, see McDonnell.

4. For an excellent summary of the arguments on both sides, see Brycchan Carey, "Where Was Olaudah Equiano Born? (and Why Does it Matter?)."

5. For a collection of interesting takes on African identities and cultures in relation to Equiano's text, see Korieh.

6. Given my focus on redefining American identity, my use of "Englishman" here might seem strange. But I would nonetheless connect this new, transatlantic identity of Equiano's very much to America and the New World, not only in the kinds of symbolic ways on which my overall arguments depend, but also for practical reasons. For one thing, all Americans were at this time still English subjects. Moreover, during and after the Revolution a number of the most significant founding Americans (including Franklin, Jefferson, and John Adams) likewise moved extensively to and through Europe. Tom Paine, one of the Revolution's most eloquent and impassioned supporters, was himself an emigrant from England and spent most of his post-Revolutionary life in Europe. Certainly Paine's rhetoric, like the Declaration's, argues for a full separation of America from England, but the realities of Revolutionary American identity were, on multiple levels, significantly more cross-cultural.

7. The book is most likely Thomas Wilson's *Essay towards an Instruction for the Indians* (1740), a missionary text produced for James Oglethorpe and his fellow Georgia trustees.

8. Bicknell and Day, *The Dying Negro: A Poem* 4.

9. The Revolution itself merits only the briefest aside in Equiano's narrative—he mentions a battle between "an American privateer" and his Royal Navy fleet (233)—and so the historical elision would seem mutual. But given Equiano's transatlantic experiences, I would argue that his revolutionary American identity incorporates both the United States and England, as well as the West Indies, Africa, and ports beyond; the ease with which he travels to Philadelphia and back to England in 1785 suggests that the Revolution has not altered that identity's emphasis on movement and cross-cultural encounters.

Chapter 4

1. For the contexts of the Harris quote, see Bertuca et al., xxiv. A similar, if somewhat more nuanced, perspective on the relationship of American expansion to Native American cultures was more famously articulated at the exposition by Frederick Jackson Turner in his address "The Significance of the Frontier in American History."

2. See also Carpenter; and Tisinger. For one of Pratt's fullest definitions of the contact zone concept, see Pratt 6–7. For other readings of European and native relationships through the lens of contact, see Frank; Barr; Preston.

3. Although Winnemucca published the book under her married name, Sarah Winnemucca Hopkins, I refer to her throughout by her maiden name, as has been the custom in scholarship. Similarly, while she spells her tribe's name "Piute," I use the current accepted spelling of Paiute when not quoting her words.

4. Jefferson cites Logan to illustrate Native Americans' "eminence in oratory," including a paragraph-long quotation from the Chief's speech to Lord Dunmore; in that passage, interestingly enough, Logan emphasizes his own cross-cultural gestures, his feeding and clothing of all those whites who "entered Logan's cabin" in need. Jefferson, *Notes on the State of Virginia* 188–89.

5. It is likely (but impossible to verify) that the band in question was the Donner Party, whose famously tragic and gruesome experiences took place in the Sierra Nevada mountains during the winter of 1846 to 1847.

6. Contemporary readers would likely know, from Winnemucca's married name of Hopkins and perhaps as well from awareness of her biography, that she subsequently validated this romantic open-mindedness by marrying the white Indian official and reformer Lewis Hopkins. She has already mentioned Hopkins once, in an aside at the outset of chapter 5, and concludes the narrative with a brief statement of their marriage.

Chapter 5

1. For a number of recent scholarly takes on Anzaldúa, see Keating. For an application of the concept of "cultural and racial *mestizaje*" (1), see Contreras.

2. One could argue that Anzaldúa's "we" here refers more to Chicano than American culture, and perhaps she herself would have claimed that as the primary association. But I read her text as ultimately focused on the presences and connections of these hybrid, cross-cultural, alternative identities across any static cultural borders and so see this chapter's alternative history as bridging those gaps. Similarly, I do not analyze the ongoing and certainly central element of gender in Anzaldúa's text—there is no question that her "we" is often explicitly gendered, but I again would argue that at their heart, her ideas and text seek to challenge and bridge, rather than reinforce, boundaries between genders, sexual identities and preferences, and the like.

Conclusion

1. See Kakutani. Remnick used Lewis's statement as the starting point (and title) for his recent biography of Obama, *The Bridge: The Life and Rise of Barack Obama.*
2. Video of Beck's characterization is available at numerous sites; see "Fox Host Glenn Beck." For Limbaugh on "reparations," see Benin.. For a representative take on Sotomayor, see "Sonia Sotomayor.".
3. For the meaning of Obama's census choice, see for example Avila.
4. For a sample connection to Douglass, see Cohen. Connections to King were widespread, including Michelle Bernard's comment, on MSNBC's *Hardball with Chris Matthews,* that the speech was "the best speech and most important speech on race that we have heard as a nation since Martin Luther King's 'I Have a Dream' speech.".
5. For a number of such takes on the "grandmother moment," see Muir.
6. Obama ends the preface by acknowledging that he might have "written a different book," one focused more on his mother's equally extraordinary life and transformations. But in any case, he admits, she was "the single constant in [his] life," and thus her identity and transformations were without question profound influences on his own (xii).
7. For clarity, I refer throughout to Obama's father as "Barack" and to Obama by his last name.
8. For an article that both includes this Romney quote and connects it to Jesse Jackson's equally limiting racial definitions of Obama, see Schaeffer.
9. For an account of a few such speeches and their responses, see Feldman.
10. See for example Henderson.
11. "Relatively small" is perhaps overly optimistic; in an August 2010 CNN/Opinion Research poll, 11% of respondents believed Obama "definitely" to have been born outside of the United States, while another 16% believed he "probably" was born elsewhere.

Works Cited

Alcoff, Linda Mártin, et al., eds. *Identity Politics Reconsidered*. New York: Palgrave Macmillan, 2006. Print.

Anzaldúa, Gloria. *Borderlands/La Frontera: The New Mestiza*. 1987. San Francisco: Aunt Lute, 1999. Print.

Armstrong, Nancy, and Leonard Tennenhouse. *The Imaginary Puritan: Literature, Intellectual Labor, and the Origins of Personal Life*. Berkeley: U of California P, 1992. Print.

Augenbraum, Harold, and Margarita Fernández Olmos, eds. *The Latino Reader: An American Literary Tradition from 1542 to the Present*. New York: Houghton, 1997. Print.

Baym, Nina, ed. *Norton Anthology of American Literature*. 7th ed. New York: Norton, 2007. Print.

———, ed. *Norton Anthology of American Literature*. Shorter 7th ed. New York: Norton, 2007. Print.

Beinert, Peter. "Is Barack Obama American Enough?" *Time*. 9 Oct. 2008. Web 8 June 2010. <http://www.time.com/time/magazine/article/0,9171,1848755,00.html>.

Benin, Steve. "Limbaugh, Health Care, and 'Reparations.'" *Political Animal*. Washington Monthly. 23 Feb. 2010. Web 8 June 2010. <http://www.washingtonmonthly.com/archives/individual/2010_02/022539.php>.

Bennett, William J. *To Reclaim a Legacy: A Report on the Humanities in Higher Education*. Washington, DC: National Endowment for the Humanities, 1984. Print.

Bernard, Michelle. *Hardball with Chris Matthews*. MSNBC. 19 Mar. 2008. Web 8 June 2010. <http://www.msnbc.msn.com/id/23707778/>.

Bernstein, Richard. *Dictatorship of Virtue: Multiculturalism and the Battle for America's Future*. New York: Knopf, 1994. Print.

Bertuca, David J., Donald K. Hartman, and Susan M. Neumister, eds. *The World's Columbian Exposition: A Centennial Bibliographic Guide*. Santa Barbara: Greenwood, 1996. Print.

Bicknell, John and Thomas Day. *The Dying Negro, a Poem*. 3rd ed. London: W. Flexney, 1775. Web 20 Oct. 2010. <http://www.brycchancarey.com/slavery/dying.htm/>.

Bloom, Allan. *The Closing of the American Mind: How Higher Education Has Failed Democracy and Impoverished the Souls of Today's Students*. New York: Simon & Schuster, 1987. Print.

Bourne, Randolph. "Trans-National America." *Atlantic Monthly* 118 (July 1916): 86–97. Print.

Bradford, William. Excerpts from *Of Plymouth Plantation*. Baym 7th ed. 58–80.

Buisseret, David, and Steven G. Reinhardt, eds. *Creolization in the Americas*. College Station: Texas A&M UP, 2000. Print.

Cabeza de Vaca, Álvar Núñez. *The Narrative of Cabeza de Vaca*. 1542. Ed. and trans. Rolena Adorno and Patrick Charles Pautz. Lincoln: U of Nebraska P, 2003. Print.

Carbonera, Lorena. *Writing from the Contact Zone: Native American Autobiography in the Nineteenth Century*. Rome: Aracne, 2009. Print.

Carey, Brycchan. "Where Was Olaudah Equiano Born? (And Why Does it Matter?)" *Brycchan Carey's Website*. 29 June 2010. Web 18 Aug. 2009. <http://www.brycchancarey.com/equiano/nativity.htm>.

Carretta, Vincent. *Equiano, the African: Biography of a Self-Made Man*. Athens: U of Georgia P, 2005. Print.

Castiglia, Christopher. *Bound and Determined: Captivity, Culture-Crossing, and White Womanhood from Mary Rowlandson to Patty Hearst*. Chicago: U of Chicago P, 1996. Print.

Cohen, Michael. "What Does Obama Have in Common with Frederick Douglass?" *Opinion Pages*. New York Times. 17 Aug. 2008. Web 8 June 2010. <http://campaignstops.blogs.nytimes.com/2008/08/17/what-does-obama-have-in-common-with-frederick-douglass/>.

Columbus, Christopher. "Letter to Ferdinand and Isabella Regarding the Fourth Voyage." 7 July 1503. Baym, 7th ed. 13–14. Print.

———. "Letter to Luis de Santangel Regarding the First Voyage." 15 Feb. 1493. Baym, 7th ed. 11–12. Print.

Confederate Yankee. "Alien Obama." *Confederate Yankee*. 25 Sept. 2008. Web 8 June 2010. <http://confederateyankee.mu.nu/archives/274201.php>.

Dalmage, Heather M., ed. *The Politics of Multiracialism: Challenging Racial Thinking*. Albany: State U of New York P, 2004. Print.

Dippel, John V. H. *Race to the Frontier: "White Flight" and Westward Expansion*. New York: Algora, 2005. Print.

D'Souza, Dinesh. *Illiberal Education: The Politics of Race and Sex on Campus*. New York: Free Press, 1991. Print.

Equiano, Olaudah. *The Interesting Narrative of the Life of Olaudah Equiano, or, Gustavus Vassa, the African; Written by Himself*. 1794. New York: Modern Library, 2004. Print.

"Fox Host Glenn Beck: Obama is a 'Racist' (VIDEO)." *Huffington Post*. 28 July 2009. Web 8 June 2010. <http://www.huffingtonpost.com/2009/07/28/fox-host-glenn-beck-obama_n_246310.html>.

Franklin, Benjamin. "Join or Die." 1754. *APStudent.com*. n.d. Web Oct. 20, 2010. <http://www.apstudent.com/ushistory/docs1751/joindie.htm>.

Gates, Henry Louis, Jr. *Loose Canons: Notes on the Culture Wars*. New York: Oxford UP, 1992. Print.

Glissant, Eduoard. "Creolization in the Making of the Americas." Hyatt and Nettleford 268–75. Print.

Goldstein, David S. Introduction. Goldstein and Thacker. xiii–xxviii.

Goldstein, David S., and Aubrey B. Thacker, eds. *Complicating Constructions: Race, Ethnicity, and Hybridity in American Texts.* Seattle: U of Washington P, 2007. Print.

Graff, Gerald. *Beyond the Culture Wars: How Teaching the Conflicts Can Revitalize American Education.* New York: Norton, 1992. Print.

Grobman, Laurie. *Multicultural Hybridity: Transforming American Literary Scholarship and Pedagogy.* Urbana: NCTE, 2007. Print.

Harris, Dean A. Introduction. *Multiculturalism from the Margins: Non-Dominant Voices on Difference and Diversity.* Ed. Harris. Westport: Bergin, 1995. ix–xvii. Print.

Harris, J. T. Opening speech. Columbian Exposition. Chicago. 21 Oct. 1892. Bertuca et al. xxiv. Print.

Henderson, Nia-Malika. "Right Blasts Obama Speech to Students." *Politico.* 3 Sept. 2009. Web 8 June 2010. <http://www.politico.com/news/stories/0909/26711 .html>.

Hirsch, E. D., Jr. *Cultural Literacy: What Every American Needs to Know.* Boston: Houghton, 1987. Print.

Hollinger, David. *Postethnic America: Beyond Multiculturalism.* New York: Basic, 1995. Print.

Howard, David. *Conquistador in Chains: Cabeza de Vaca and the Indians of the Americas.* Tuscaloosa: U of Alabama P, 1997. Print.

Hubel, Teresa, and Neil Brooks, eds. *Literature and Racial Ambiguity.* Amsterdam: Rodopi, 2002. Print.

Hughes, Robert. *Culture of Complaint: The Fraying of America.* London: Harvill, 1994. Print.

Hunsaker, Steven V. *Autobiography and National Identity in the Americas.* Charlottesville: UP of Virginia, 1999. Print.

Hunter, James Davison. *Culture Wars: The Struggle to Define America.* New York: Basic, 1991. Print.

Hyatt, Vera Lawrence, and Rex Nettleford, eds. *Race, Discourse, and the Origins of the Americas: A New World View.* Washington, DC: Smithsonian Institution Press, 1995. Print.

Jackson, Jesse, Jr. "Jesse Jackson: Obama's 'acting like he's white.'" *Political Ticker.* CNN. 19 Sept. 2007. Web 8 June 2010. <http://politicalticker.blogs.cnn.com/2007/09/19/ jessie-jackson-obamas-acting-like-hes-white/?fbid=fopFly56SRe>.

Jefferson, Thomas. "The Declaration of Independence." *The Writings of Thomas Jefferson.* Vol. 1. By Jefferson. Washington, DC: Thomas Jefferson Memorial Assn., 1903. 28–38. Print.

———. *Notes on the State of Virginia.* New York: Library of America, 1984. Print.

Jennings, Francis. *The Invasion of America: Indians, Colonialism, and the Cant of Conquest.* Chapel Hill: U of North Carolina P, 1975. Print.

Kakutani, Michiko. "Seeking Identity, Shaping a Nation's." *New York Times.* 5 April 2010. Web Oct. 20, 2010. <http://www.nytimes.com/2010/04/06/books/06book .html>.

Kallen, Horace M. "Democracy versus the Melting Pot: A Study of American Nationality." *The Nation* 100 (18 Feb. 1915): 192–93; 100 (25 Feb. 1915): 217–20. *Pluralism and Unity.* Web 25 Aug. 2009. <http://www.expo98.msu.edu/people/Kallen.htm>.

Kingston, Maxine Hong. *China Men.* New York: Knopf, 1980. Print.

———. *The Woman Warrior: Memories of a Girlhood Among Ghosts.* New York: Knopf, 1977. Print.

Kivisto, Peter, and Georganne Rundblad, eds. *Multiculturalism in the United States: Current Issues, Contemporary Voices.* Thousand Oaks: Pine Forge Press, 2000. Print.

Klekowski, Libby. "Old Style Calendar Dating." *The Connecticut River Homepage.* U of Massachusetts Amherst. n.d. Web 21 June 2008. <http://www.bio.umass.edu/biology/conn.river/calendar.html>.

Krieger, Alex D. *We Came Naked and Barefoot: The Journey of Cabeza de Vaca across North America.* Austin: U of Texas P, 2002. Print.

Kwan, SanSan, and Kenneth Speirs, eds. *Mixing It Up: Multiracial Subjects.* Austin: U of Texas P, 2004. Print.

Langley, April C. E. *The Black Aesthetic Unbound: Theorizing the Dilemma of Eighteenth-Century African American Literature.* Columbus: Ohio State UP, 2008. Print.

Lima, Lázaro. *The Latino Body: Crisis Identities in American Literary and Cultural Memory.* New York: New York UP, 2007. Print.

McGovern, Thomas V. *Memory's Stories: Interdisciplinary Readings of Multicultural Life Narratives.* Lanham: UP of America, 2007. Print.

Morgan, Edmund. *American Slavery, American Freedom: The Ordeal of Colonial Virginia.* New York: Norton, 1975. Print.

Morgan, Lewis Henry. *Ancient Society; or, Researches in the Lines of Human Progress from Savagery, through Barbarism to Civilization.* London: McMillan, 1877. *Marxists Internet Archive.* n.d. Web. 21 Aug. 2009. <http://www.marxists.org/reference/archive/morgan-lewis/ancient-society/index.htm>.

———. *League of the Ho-De-No-Sau-Nee or Iroquois.* New York: Dodd, Mead, 1904. 1851. *Google Books.* Google. n.d. Web 21 Aug. 2009, <http://books.google.com/books?id=5usNAAAAIAAJ&dq=Lewis+Henry+Morgan&printsec=frontcover&source=an&hl=en&ei=YyBOSsm4B4j7tge95YGgBA&sa=X&oi=book_result&ct=result&resnum=8>.

Nash, Gary B. *Red, White, and Black: The Peoples of Early North America.* 6th ed. New York: Pearson, 2010.

Nettleford, Rex. Afterword. *Race, Discourse, and the Origins of the Americas: A New World View.* Ed. Vera Lawrence Hyatt and Nettleford. Washington, DC: Smithsonian Institution. 276–92. Print.

Newfield, Christopher, and Avery F. Gordon. "Multiculturalism's Unfinished Business." *Mapping Multiculturalism.* Ed. Gordon and Newfield. Minneapolis: U of Minnesota P, 1996. 76–115. Print.

Nolan, James, Jr. Preface. *The American Culture Wars: Current Contests and Future Prospects.* Ed. Nolan. Charlottesville: UP of Virginia, 1996. ix–xvi. Print.

Obama, Barack. *Dreams from My Father: A Story of Race and Inheritance.* 2nd ed. New York: Three Rivers Press, 2004. Print.

————. "A More Perfect Union." Philadelphia. 18 Mar. 2008. Web. <http://www .barackobama.com/2008/03/18/remarks_of_senator_barack_obam_53.php>.

Pratt, Mary Louise. *Imperial Eyes: Travel Writing and Transculturation.* London: Routledge, 1992. Print.

Reed, Ishmael, ed. *Multi-America: Essays on Cultural Wars and Cultural Peace.* New York: Viking, 1997. Print.

Reed-Danahay, Deborah E., ed. *Auto/Ethnography: Rewriting the Self and the Social.* Oxford: Berg, 1997. Print.

Rifkin, Mark. *Manifesting America: The Imperial Construction of U.S. National Space.* New York: Oxford UP, 2009. Print.

Roof, Wade Clark. "'I Want My Country Back!': The Demography of Discontent." *Religion Dispatches.* 30 Sept. 2009. Web 8 June 2010. <http://www .religiondispatches.org/archive/politics/1864/%E2%80%9Ci_want_my _country_back!%E2%80%9D%3A_the_demography_of_discontent>.

Rosen, Harold. *Speaking from Memory: A Guide to Autobiographical Acts and Practices.* Oakhill: Trentham, 1998. Print.

Rosenwald, Lawrence. *Multilingual America: Language and the Making of American Literature.* Cambridge: Cambridge UP, 2008. Print.

Rowlandson, Mary. *The Narrative of the Captivity and Restoration of Mrs. Mary Rowlandson.* Boston: Houghton, 1930. Print. Originally published as *The Sovereignty and Goodness of God.* London: Joseph Poole, 1682.

Schlesinger, Arthur M., Jr. *The Disuniting of America: Reflections on a Multicultural Society.* New York: Norton, 1992. Print.

Schmidt, Alvin J. *The Menace of Multiculturalism: Trojan Horse in America.* Westport: Praeger, 1997. Print.

Senier, Siobhan. *Voices of American Indian Assimilation and Resistance: Helen Hunt Jackson, Sarah Winnemucca, and Victoria Howard.* Norman: U of Oklahoma P, 2001. Print.

Shoemaker, Nancy. *A Strange Likeness: Becoming Red and White in Eighteenth-Century North America.* New York: Oxford UP, 2004. Print.

Silver, Peter. *Our Savage Neighbors: How Indian War Transformed Early America.* New York: Norton, 2008. Print.

Smith, Barbara Herrnstein. "Cult-Lit: Hirsch, Literacy, and the 'National Culture.'" *South Atlantic Quarterly* 89.1 (Winter 1990): 69–88. Print.

Smith, Sidonie, and Julia Watson. *Reading Autobiography: A Guide for Interpreting Life Narratives.* Minneapolis: U of Minnesota P, 2001. Print.

Sokolow, Jayme A. *The Great Encounter: Native Peoples and European Settlers in the Americas, 1492–1800.* Armonk: Sharpe, 2003. Print.

Sollors, Werner. *Beyond Ethnicity: Consent and Descent in American Culture.* New York: Oxford UP, 1986. Print.

————. "A Critique of Pure Pluralism." *Reconstructing American Literary History.* Ed. Sacvan Bercovitch Cambridge, MA: Harvard UP, 1986. 250–79. Print.

————, ed. *Multilingual America: Transnationalism, Ethnicity, and the Languages of American Literature.* New York: New York UP, 1998. Print.

————. *Neither Black nor White yet Both: Thematic Explorations of Interracial Literature.* New York: Oxford UP, 1997. Print.

Sommer, Doris. *Bilingual Aesthetics: A New Sentimental Education.* Durham: Duke UP, 2004. Print.

————, ed. *Bilingual Games: Some Literary Investigations.* New York: Palgrave Mac-Millan, 2003. Print.

"Sonia Sotomayor: Affirmative Action Nominee for Supreme Court? Close to Far-Left Puerto Rico Extremists?" *24Ahead.com: Immigration and Politics.* n.d. Web 8 June 2010. <http://24ahead.com/sonia-sotomayor-affirmative-action-nominee-supreme-court-clo>.

Spengemann, William C. *The Forms of Autobiography: Episodes in the History of a Literary Genre.* New Haven: Yale UP, 1980. Print.

Springsteen, Bruce. "American Skin (41 Shots)." *Bruce Springsteen and the E Street Band: Live in New York City.* Sony, 2001. CD.

Takaki, Ronald. *A Different Mirror: A History of Multicultural America.* Boston: Little, 1993. Print.

Travis, Shannon. "Quarter doubt Obama was born in U.S." *Political Ticker.* CNN. 4 Aug. 2010. Web 10 Aug. 2010. <http://politicalticker.blogs.cnn.com/2010/08/04/cnn-poll-quarter-doubt-president-was-born-in-u-s/?fbid=tS8Z4934mGR>.

Turner, Frederick Jackson. "The Significance of the Frontier in American History." American Historical Association. Chicago. July 12, 1893. *xroads: The American Studies Hypertexts Project.* 30 Sept. 1997. Web Oct. 20, 2010. <http://xroads.virginia.edu/~hyper/turner/>.

Van Zandt, Cynthia J. *Brothers among Nations: The Pursuit of Intercultural Alliances in Early America, 1580–1660.* New York: Oxford UP, 2008. Print.

Wallsten, Peter. "Frank Talk of Obama and Race in Virginia." *Los Angeles Times.* 25 Oct. 2008. Web 8 June 2010. <http://articles.latimes.com/2008/oct/05/nation/na-virginia5>.

Waters, Mary C. "Multiple Ethnic Identity Choices." *Beyond Pluralism: The Conception of Groups and Group Identities in America.* Ed. Wendy F. Katkin, Ned Landsman, and Andrea Tyree. Urbana: U of Illinois P, 1998. 28–46. Print.

Wheatley, Phillis. "On Being Brought from Africa to America." 1773. Baym, shorter ed. 420–21. Print.

————. "To His Excellency, General Washington." 1775. Baym, shorter ed. 427–28. Print.

————. "To the Right Honorable William, Earl of Dartmouth." 1773. Baym, shorter ed. 428–29. Print.

Winnemucca Hopkins, Sarah. *Life among the Piutes: Their Wrongs and Claims.* Boston: Cupples, 1883. Print.

Zanjani, Sally. *Sarah Winnemucca.* Lincoln: U of Nebraska P, 2001. Print.

Zinn, Howard. *A People's History of the United States.* London: Longman, 1980. Print.

Further Reading

Avila, Oscar. "Obama's Census Choice: Simply African-American." *Chicago Break-ingNewsCenter.* 2 Apr. 2010. Web 8 June 2010. <http://www.chicagobreaking news.com/2010/04/obamas-census-choice-simply-african-american.html>.

Barr, Daniel P., ed. *The Boundaries between Us: Natives and Newcomers along the Frontiers of the Old Northwest Territory, 1750–1850.* Kent: Kent State UP, 2006. Print.

Burnham, Michelle. *Captivity and Settlement: Cultural Exchange in American Literature, 1682–1891.* Hanover: UP of New England, 1997. Print.

Carpenter, Cari. "Tiresias Speaks: Sarah Winnemucca's Hybrid Selves and Genres." *Legacy* 19.1 (2002): 71–80. Print.

Contreras, Sheila Marie. *Blood Lines: Myth, Indigenism, and Chicana/o Literature.* Austin: U of Texas P, 2008. Print.

Dillon, Elizabeth Maddock. "Religion and Geopolitics in the New World." *Early American Literature* 45.1 (Winter 2010): 193–202. Print.

Egerton, Douglas. *Death or Liberty: African Americans and Revolutionary America.* New York: Oxford UP, 2009. Print.

Feldman, Jeffrey. "Is Palin Trying To Incite Violence Against Obama?" *Huffington Post.* 7 Oct. 2008. Web 8 June 2010. <http://www.huffingtonpost.com/ jeffrey-feldman/is-palin-trying-to-incite_b_132534.html>.

Frank, Andrew. *Creeks and Southerners: Biculturalism on the Early American Frontier.* Lincoln: U of Nebraska P, 2005. Print.

Gilroy, Paul. *The Black Atlantic: Modernity and Double Consciousness.* Cambridge: Harvard UP, 1993. Print.

Goodman, Nan. "'Money Answers All Things': Rethinking Economic and Cultural Exchange in the Captivity Narrative of Mary Rowlandson." *American Literary History* 22.1 (Spring 2010): 1–25. Print.

Keating, AnaLouise, ed. *EntreMundos/AmongWorlds: New Perspectives on Gloria E. Anzaldúa.* New York: Palgrave Macmillan, 2005. Print.

Korieh, Chima J., ed. *Olaudauh Equiano and the Igbo World: History, Society, and Atlantic Diaspora Connections.* Trenton: Africa World Press, 2009. Print.

Kupperman, Karen Ordahl. *Indians and English: Facing Off in Early America.* Ithaca: Cornell UP, 2000. Print.

———. *Settling with the Indians: The Meeting of English and Indian Cultures in America, 1580–1640.* Totowa: Rowman, 1980. Print.

McDonnell, Michael A. *The Politics of War: Race, Class, and Conflict in Revolutionary Virginia.* Chapel Hill: U of North Carolina P, 2007. Print.

Muir, Chris. "Barack Obama Watch: Throwing Grandma under the Bus." *FullosseousFlap's Dental Blog.* 19 Mar. 2008. Web 8 June 2010. <http://flapsblog .com/2008/03/19/barack-obama-watch-throwing-grandma-under-the-bus/>.

Preston, David L. *The Texture of Contact: European and Indian Settler Communities on the Frontiers of Iroquoia, 1667–1783.* Lincoln: U of Nebraska P, 2009. Print.

Rennick. David. *The Bridge: The Life and Rise of Barack Obama.* New York: Knopf, 2010. Print.

Schaeffer, Frank. "'Real Americans' Are Stupid! Obama vs. Mitt Romney and Jesse Jackson." *Huffington Post*. 13 July 2008. Web 8 June 2010. <http://www.huffing tonpost.com/frank-schaeffer/real-americans-are-stupid_b_112416.html>.

Sobel, Mechal. *The World They Made Together: Black and White Values in Eigh-teenth-Century Virginia*. Princeton: Princeton UP, 1987. Print.

Tisinger, Danielle. "Textual Performance and the Western Frontier: Sarah Winnemucca Hopkins' *Life Among the Piutes: Their Wrongs and Claims*." *Western American Literature* 37.2 (2002): 171–94. Print.

Wilson, Thomas. *Essay towards an Instruction for the Indians*. 1740. *Project Canterbury*. n.d. Web 18 Aug. 2009. <http://anglicanhistory.org/lact/wilson/4/index .html>.

Index